Making Short Films with ZERO-BUDGET: A Complete Guide

By Rizan Production House

Contents

CHAPTER 01: INTRODUCTION

Introduction

What are short films?

While the obvious answer is that they are shorter versions of feature length narrative films. The Academy of Motion Picture Arts and Sciences provides the following definition:

"an original motion picture that has a running time of 40 minutes or less, including all credits".

Although, short films can be up to 40 minutes long. In reality, the vast majority are far shorter than this, in fact it is fairly rare to see short films which exceed the 20 minute mark. In fact, when it comes to submitting to film festivals or even just grabbing an audience's attention, as long as you can convey the message and told the story that you have set out to, generally speaking the shorter the film, the better! No body is a fan of filler for the sake of it, regardless of whether you are watching a short or full length feature film.

Short films are usually lower in budget, although it is not unheard of to see a few short films at the larger film festivals which have budgets running into the millions of dollars. As a result of having lower budgets, they usually have fewer actors and are made with a smaller crew. Due to the time constraints, short films with also have simpler plots, and will utilise fewer locations.

Why make short films?

But if my goal is to be a feature length film maker, shouldn't I just make feature length films? Filmmakers usually have that one key project in the back of their mind which is going to help them break into the film industry, of which they have a burning desire to get started on.

And I get the logic, but there are a whole host of reasons why you shouldn't just jump into making feature length movies straight away.

First and foremost, making short films ('shorts') is a great way to get started. It can be a fantastic way of learning the ropes and maximising what you can learn, whilst at the same time minimising the potential risks.

Consider it from this perspective. Making a feature is a time consuming and expensive process. You're better off making your mistakes now, instead of being half way through your feature and learning that there are better lighting techniques which can drastically improve your cinematography. What do you do in that scenario? Either be wildly inconsistent with one half of your feature looking a lot more aesthetic and having an inconsistent picture or continue with your old techniques and be unhappy with the final product? Make your mistakes on your shorts. It will save you time, headaches and heartaches later on.

Like I mentioned, features are also very expensive. You don't want to sink a lot of money into making your feature, only to realise that you could have done a lot better and you end up with a final product which you are ashamed of. Practise makes perfect. Shorts are a great way to practice.

Regardless of where you are in your filmmaking journey, creating a short can be a great way to improve your technical ability. Regardless of whether you are just starting out or whether you've been in the game for a while and just want to practice using certain techniques a bit more, shorts are a relatively efficient way of doing so. Testing out new ideas in the context of a narrative story will make the difference between a great technical cameraman and a filmmaker.

In other words, making a short is the equivalent of taking swimming lessons before jumping into the sea. It may seem like a pain at the time, but you'll be glad you took the time to properly learn.

Creating shorts can also help you to establish and/or grow your filmmaking network. The age old saying of it's not what you know, but who you know is applicable more so in filmmaking than anywhere else. The connections you have can make or break your career. This can be done in two ways, firstly you may end up working with a great team which results in you creating the project which helps you become recognised and launches your careers. Or alternatively, one of the individuals who you work with ends up making it, and recommends your name for any future projects. Do not underestimate the power of a strong network. Shorts are a great way to meet up with other like minded individuals, across a range of roles ranging from camera operators, sound engineers, producers, composers, actors etc. operating within your local area who you can collaborate with. Working with those you are more experienced than you can be a great way to learn in a practical and efficient manner.

Once you have a number of great shorts under your belt, you can create a show reel for your work. This can be invaluable in persuading other, talented peers to work with you on your projects.

Furthermore, once you have completed a number of shorts, this can help build a reputation for yourself in the filmmaking community which can lead to other opportunities coming your way. It also creates a solid fan base and a certain "buzz" around your name which can be a great marketing tool, regardless of whether you are just distributing online or submitting to film festivals. Especially when you are pitching for funding in the future for your feature, if the investors know that you are bringing a base audience with you, even before any marketing has been done, this will make the venture less risky and thus more attractive to investors.

But what if I've done a number of shorts, I'm happy with my technical ability and have a great idea for a feature? Makes sense to jump straight into the feature, right? Maybe. There still may be opportunity to create one final short. And perhaps the most important one to date.

Shorts can also be used to validate feature films, by creating a shorter version of the story and using this is a marketing and research tool before committing to your feature length film. This is known as a proof in concept. It is a great way of figuring out whether audiences are interested in the subject matter of your feature and the style you wish to present the feature in. There is nothing worse than spending stupid amounts of time and money on a film that only you are interested in, unless of course, you have money to burn. You want to ensure that an audience is out there for your film, before you commit the time and money needed for your feature film. A proof in concept can help you decide whether to go ahead with a project, and if so, how to approach it. This can be invaluable and save you months of headache.

Why are you advocating making shorts for free?

One factor which amateur filmmakers often find discouraging is the price tag that often comes with many short films. If you look up the major film festival winners, in the short film category, over recent years, it is clear that many of the winners are working with huge budgets in the hundreds of thousands and potentially even millions. It is easy to look at these films and feel discouraged, as it will be near impossible to compete with these films if your aim is to gain recognition through the film festival route. And it's true. There are companies spending hundreds of thousands, and sometimes millions, on their short films. And yes, companies with dedicated VFX teams often do win in their respective categories at major film festivals.

But there are still a ton of festivals which target individuals making shorts for little to no budget, which can still help you get noticed by the right people. Heck, with an engaging enough story, there is nothing stopping you from getting shortlisted and winning major festivals too. Not all winners in recent years have had huge budgets.

If money was all it took to create great films, Hollywood would have no terrible movies. And we all know that this isn't true.

Aside from gaining a buzz, the main objective of creating short films for most is to practice their craft, both in terms of technical aspects and their ability to tell a story. This can be done with limited equipment and cast, and definitely for free. Framing it another way - why spend money making mistakes when you can make them for free?

Another thing to consider that is, short films rarely make their money back, unlike feature films, as there isn't really a market for them.

No one goes to the cinema or a streaming
service to watch short movies (well, rarely
anyway, and only if a major director or actor is
attached). So any money invested is lost,
unless you get headhunted as a result of it
reaching the right people, which is incredibly
rare, although does happen from time to time.

You are better off saving the money, to use
later on your debut feature film, which is far
more likely to get picked up by distributors.
As a result, it is also more likely to launch
your filmmaking career, and make all or some
of your money back - and dare I say it, even
make a profit!

CHAPTER 02: CAMERA EQUIPMENT

Camera Equipment

Do I need a cinema grade camera?

The number one obstacle that holds amateur filmmakers back is gear envy.

Although it may sound ridiculous, the number one excuse that's often thrown around is that you can't possibly be taken seriously as a professional, unless you've got professional level gear.

And whilst this will be true to an extent at a higher level, most of us are not at that level yet. And better gear does NOT result in better films. It may result in more cinematic footage, but to be completely honest, most audiences are forgiving of a slight decrease in picture quality in exchange for a fantastic story.

By stating that you're bottleneck for making greater films is equipment is basically saying that you've maxed out your potential in all other areas. I can assure you that this is not the case for virtually every amateur filmmaker. Even without a great camera, there is much to be learnt as to the most effective way to tell a great story and engage an audience. This should be your focus over the first few years, rather than the codec capabilities of your camera.

While you are still learning, focus on all the intangible points you are able to improve upon. If the eventual goal is to be a fulltime director on large budget feature films, you will not be micro managing the camera or boom pole anyhow, this will be delegated to more technical members of staff. It is your job to tell the story and make sure everything comes together. This is what you should be practising, everything else is secondary.

If you are reading this book, I will assume that most of you will have a camera and hence will not add it as an expense. If you have a camera, no matter how basic, use this. There is no need to purchase something more expensive or flashier for the time being. Even if you don't have a dedicated video camera, a smart phone or tablet can be just as good in the right hands. Most of us would rather watch a great story shot on a smart phone, than a film with an awful premise and execution shot on an Arri Alexa.

If you are still not convinced by my explanation and insist on purchasing a dedicated video camera, then I have provided a few pointers below. However, note that I still stand that this is unnecessary.

Buy a video camera which is outdated, without the latest technology and second hand but still in decent condition. You do not need the latest image stabilisation or viewfinder. Just something which can film a video will do for now. The best place to get a great discount is usually through family and friends who are looking to get rid of their old items, car boot sales (make sure to test the camera works), online on sites like Ebay, Gumtree and Amazon or through selling pages on social media. Or if you have the option, borrow a camera from someone you know for your projects, as long as you know you will take good care of it.

A good option is one of the older DSLR's. For example the Canon Rebel T3i, or Canon EOS 600D depending on which part of the world you live in, is often cited as a fantastic camera for beginners. Whilst the technology is over a decade old and there are certainly better cameras out there now, it provides everything you need at the entry level and is a great way to learn about the technical aspects of video such as frame rates, ISO, aperture etc. Plus, with it being so old and common, it can be found incredibly cheap online for as little as $150 - $200, with a kit lens.

However it is worth noting that this is not a dedicated video camera and is aimed at photographers. This does not mean it is not a great camera for beginner filmmakers. However, if you want something you can grow into, a mirrorless camera such as the Panasonic Lumix G7 might be a good option. It is newer and as a result more expensive, however it has many benefits over a DSLR camera, such as the Canon Rebel T3i, such as having the ability to shoot videos in 4K, focus peaking, touch screen display etc. Do some research and find out what is best for you.

However, if you are a complete beginner, as I mentioned earlier, you do not even need a dedicated video camera. Most of us will have a smart phone or a tablet available to them, which allows us to take videos. This is sufficient during the beginning stages of learning to make short films. As mentioned earlier, your limiting factor during the beginning stages won't be the equipment, it will be your ability to tell a story. In fact, by limiting your equipment, your forced to focus more on the story and think like a director - something which will come in handy as more expensive equipment eventually finds its way over to you. You can always upgrade your equipment once you feel you have outgrown what you are currently using, it is more important to get started.

Don't believe me? Check out Tangerine, a film created by Sean Baker in 2015 which had huge critical success. The film was short entirely on an iPhone 5S. It premiered at the prestigious Sundance Film Festival, and managed to gain enough traction for it to be picked up by

Magnolia Pictures. It then went on to make $925k at the box office. Not bad for a film shot on a smart phone, right?

There are also many advantages to shooting with a phone or tablet which you would not usually have with more professional cameras. For example, there are less bulky and easier to shoot in more tight spaces, they can be set up quicker and are therefore more suited to guerrilla filmmaking, they're portable and therefore easier to shoot multiple locations with on a single day and carry around.

On the other hand, they're obviously not perfect. The image quality is decent, however it clearly can't compete with an Arri Alexa - although this shouldn't be your focus when starting out. It also won't help teach you about technical aspects of certain cameras, however this will come in time once you upgrade.

Weigh up and pros and cons and make a decision for yourself.

Digital vs. Film

If you have been active in the film community, you will know that a continuous debate that is going on between filmmakers is whether to shoot with digital cameras or to shoot via the more traditional route on film stock. I will not go into too much detail, as I could write an entire book on this topic alone, but just briefly touch on the subject.

Let's get one thing out of the way. Film is undeniably sexy. There are no two ways about it. There is a certain mystical aura to shooting on film, which makes you feel like an old school filmmaker, like Stanley Kubrick or Alfred Hitchcock. It is well respected amongst the filmmaking community, and seen as producing superior image quality to digital, as it adds a certain texture to your footage which digital cannot quite capture.

So, this means we should all be shooting on film, right?

Well, not quite. In fact, I would argue that as an amateur filmmaker just starting out, you should stay away from film entirely and stick to digital, for now at least.

For starters, film is expensive. It is not only expensive to purchase, but it is also expensive to process. Then there is the storage costs, as overtime film is liable to degrade, you need to ensure it is stored correctly. As an amateur filmmaker, you are unlikely to have the money to make short film after short film using film stock.

Film is also more technically difficult to work with. It requires its own set of cameras, and is a pain to work with in low light conditions, compared to new digital cameras. You will really need to study how much light is required and the distances you need to place your cameras at etc. As you are just starting out, you are already having to learn a lot. Adding all the technical requirements of shooting on film into the mix can be incredibly overwhelming for a newcomer.

To clarify, this is not me saying that you should avoid film throughout your entire filmmaking career. However, it is something you may should consider easing yourself into,

rather than diving into head first just as you
are starting out.

Lenses

Unless you've got a dedicated video camera,
this section does not apply to you so feel free
to skip ahead.

After cameras, the second piece of gear which
everyone obsesses over is lenses.

Yes, filmmakers use varying lenses to get their
desired effect. And yes, you will eventually
need to learn about the different effects of
using varying focal lengths.

However, lenses can be VERY expensive, often
times even more expensive than the camera
body. They are probably the one piece of
equipment which hasn't come down in price
over the years, because they are complex and
difficult to make!

If you purchased a beginner camera, chances
are that it came with a kit lens. Now, some
people love to discourage others when it
comes to using the kits lens. I couldn't

disagree more. While I acknowledge that
they're usually flimsy and not manufactured
to last, as well as not having the sharpest
image quality. They do have some advantages,
such as being ridiculously good value for
money for what you are getting. The image
quality is still incredible, even if it does not
match that of professional grade cameras, they
usually are multiple times more expensive.
They are also zoom lenses which, although not
ideal for cinematic filmmaking, are great for
beginners as it can help you decide which
focal lengths you like the look of and which
you wish to use to tell your story best.

Zoom lenses also have the advantage of being
more flexible, in terms of you being able to just
turn a dial to change your focal length.
Compare this to prime lenses which require
you to physically move if you want to change
how far the subject is from the camera. Prime
lenses are often the preferred choice for
filmmakers, as they provide a sharper image.
But as mentioned earlier, this is not a priority.
You can pick up prime lenses further into your
career.

And yes, cinematic lenses do exist. However,
they are so expensive that they aren't even
worth acknowledging at this stage of your
career. Unless you are a professional, you will
not need cinematic lenses, and at this stage
you will look to rent them.

CHAPTER 03: LIGHTING

Lighting

Beginners always wonder what the secret to creating the perfect cinematic look is. What is it that separates their images to that of other amateur filmmakers who have similar equipment but a far superior end result? That can be answered in one simple word: lighting. Good lighting can drastically transform your images, and it is well worth the time to learn how to do it right.

Lighting is a key technical skill that most cinematographers seek to master. That knowledge is often why Hollywood is willing to pay them the big bucks. They can combine technical knowledge with creative flair to produce the desired outcome.

Lighting is considered in depth for every shot you see on the big screen. Even shots which are seemingly shot with natural lights often aren't. Instead, they are supplemented or even sometimes entirely replaced by artificial lighting in order to recreate the natural light look. This seems bizarre and you're right to question why this is done. It can be used to soften harsh shadows or create the look for a certain time of day. For example, if you have a long scene set for a certain time in the day, you cannot rely solely on the sun which is temperamental and will be brighter at certain times of the day, thus giving you varying shadow lengths. Using artificial lights, cinematographers are able to get a consistent look throughout the full shooting day.

However, lighting isn't cheap. Specialised film lights usually cost hundreds and can even run into the thousands. However, luckily there are two quick workarounds for this issue.

Please note that I will not teach specific lighting techniques in this book, as this is not its intended purpose. Instead I will be discussing how to source lighting equipment, and use lighting in the most budget friendly way possible.

Indoor lighting

Firstly, instead of using lighting specifically manufactured for filmmakers, you can purchase every day lamps and outdoors lights and try and achieve a similar effect. Let me be clear, once you are in the more advanced stages of your career, dedicated filmmaking lights definitely have their merits. A lot of the dedicated filmmaking lights are not portable, powerful and are variable in the sense that the brightness and colour (which allows you to create different moods for your scenes) can be changed from any smart device. These lights are great for convenience, however you are able to achieve a similar effect on a budget, as long as you are willing to put in slightly more effort.

As a beginner making short films, use the light you have available to you. Perhaps you have multiple lamps scattered throughout your house. Great. Prop these up on a stand and use them as part of your lighting set up. Lamps work much better than traditional overhead lighting found in most houses, as these look unnatural and result in harsh shadows, which isn't very flattering towards your actors.

Instead, with lamps you can place them in differing angles, depending on the layout of your location, to create shadows and lights as you please. The look you will want to achieve will depend on the genre you are working in and the mood you wish to convey. There are plenty of online resources which you can use as a starting guide to learning lighting theory, however I would only recommend using these as a starting point - don't be afraid to experiment continuously to achieve the look you desire. Get creative and try different things out. This is the very essence of independent film making.

You will probably also require a powerful key light. If you have any outdoor LED lights from garden centres, these often work fantastically as a substitute for film lights, as they can be incredibly powerful and are not prone to overheating. Purchasing LED lighting from DIY stores will be considerably cheaper than purchasing dedicated film lights, and if you know what you are doing, the results can end up being similar.

One problem you may encounter from using such powerful lights is that you may end up with a harsh light, which results in harsh shadows on your actors. To remedy this, you would usually purchase a soft box which helps diffuse the light and make it more even. However, if you are working to a budget, a good replacement for a soft box is a bed sheet or a shower curtain. Place this onto your LED light (with a bit of distance, even though LED lights are not known to overheat, it is best to be safe).

The LED lights will also only give out light in one colour, a bright yellow/white light. If you are trying to recreate a certain feel to your scene, you may wish to tint your lights to a slightly different colour. The easiest way to do this is to purchase some coloured lighting gels which you can place over your lights or soft box. These come in many different colours, for example if you wish to convey intimacy and warmth in a scene, you may wish to use an orange colour gel which audiences usually associate with warmth. Lighting gels are usually incredibly affordable, for example a pack of 10 different colours can be purchased for under $10. However, if you are not in a position to purchase lighting gels, you can always colour grade your scene in post production to achieve a similar look.

The second method I would recommend involves using what is free to absolutely everyone - sunlight. This should be approached differently depending on whether you are shooting indoors or outdoors.

If you are shooting indoors, windows are your best friend. They are a great source of natural light and when used in conjunction with other lights (e.g. lamps), they can create a really cinematic effect. A good tip is also to use doorways to let in light from other windows throughout the house. Of course this will depend on the setup of your location, but play around and see what works best with the space you are shooting in.

Outdoor lighting

The other alternative is shooting outdoors. This may seem as simple as taking the camera outside and starting to film, but the end result often isn't great. This is mainly due to the light being too harsh which can create a poor image. There is also the issue of light moving throughout the day, creating uneven shadows. This can be problematic for scenes which take place in a short time schedule.

With money, these issues can be solved with an ND filter. An ND filter is basically sunglasses for your camera, it makes everything an even, slightly darker colour. A good tip if you are purchasing an ND filter is to purchase one which is slightly bigger than your largest lens, as long as it is variable, it should then fit on all of your lenses.

However, as we are aiming making a short film for free, if purchasing an ND filter isn't an option for you, a way around it is to ensure your shooting schedule takes into account the change of light throughout the day. This can require a lot of effort on your part, however it just requires solid organisation skills. For example, you could split the working day based on your scenes, and shooting outdoor scenes between 10am-12pm and the remainder of the day, shooting all your indoor scenes.

Alternatively, you can shoot outdoors and make use of more shaded areas, which should prevent the uneven shadows. Although this is only if you can shoot somewhere large enough which is entirely in the shade. You may also run into the issue of this area needing artificial light to brighten up the image.

If you are looking to shoot during the most cinematic time, this will as the sun is first coming up or going down each day, as this produces even sunlight and makes everything look incredible. These times of the day are what is knows in the filmmaking community as 'Golden Hour'. Of course, this comes with the disadvantage of only being able to shoot for 2 or so hours a day, but if you have time on your hands, it is definitely worth it.

However, I will go on to say that you shouldn't worry too much about shadows varying throughout the day. There have been plenty of large budget feature films who completely ignore the varying sun position, shadows and light throughout its scenes. Whilst film geeks will spot these instantly, as long as you have an engaging story, most audiences won't notice or care.

If you can avoid it, I would stay away from shooting night time scenes until you get some experience of lighting under your belt. Night time scenes are notoriously difficult to light correctly. If you are planning to shoot a lot at night, it may be worth considering whether to invest in a camera which specialises in low light. There are plenty of digital cameras which have amazing low light capabilities at very affordable prices. As a general rule, stay away from camera's with cropped lenses, as this means that they are able to take in less light than a full lens camera, which is a disadvantage during scenes with low lighting i.e. night scenes.

The key to shooting great night scenes on a budget is to make use of areas with plenty of lighting around. I know this sounds counterintuitive, but think about night scenes in popular films, often they are shot in areas with plenty of lighting such as fun fares or near shopping centres with most shops having some sort of lighting. Alternatively, you can bring some lighting equipment with you and place it on a stand or an elevated area to light your subjects up. Trying to shoot a night scene without some sort of artificial light will result in an extremely dark image where you may just about be able to make out the subject. Audiences do not want to be straining their eyes, trying to figure out what is happening in the scene.

If you are working in a location which doesn't have any artificial lights, you will have to bring the light with you. However, try and replicate the lighting you would normally find at this time of night e.g. street lamps, as this will create a more authentic look for the audience. Hollywood often likes to colour grade night light as being more blue, compared to orange which is more of a daytime look. An easy way to artificially recreate this is to bring some colour gels which are relatively cheap to buy and place them over your LED lights. This way you've got a more blue light, rather than an orange one. You can always colour grade this to be more blue in post production if it is not quite the right colour.

An alternative to shooting at night is 'day for night shooting'. This is sort of cheating in a way as you are not actually shooting at night, but shooting your scenes in the daytime and using in-camera tricks and post production techniques to make your scene appear as if it is being shot at night. However, don't feel too bad about using this technique to 'cheat' as this method is even popular amongst Hollywood blockbusters, such as Castaway, Lawrence of Arabia and Mad Max: Fury Road. There are many detailed articles on shooting day for night online, note that there is no set in stone technique as there are many ways of achieving the desired look, however the basics can be summarised as follows:

- Use an ND filter, which can be used to underexpose the image;

- Use a Polarizer, this is used to manage the hot spots in the sky and get rid of any unwanted glare;

- Use a Day For Night filter can be used to remove certain colours, such as the colour red, which gives more of a cool, blue, moonlit feel to the scene;

- Aim to shoot during times of the day
  when light is naturally lower anyway. It
  will be fairly obvious if you are trying
  to Day For Night a scene for midday
  due to the way the shadows fall.
  However, as it is already fairly dark at
  dusk or dawn, this will work to your
  advantage due to street lamps being on,
  headlights being used etc. which help
  give the scene a more natural feel. Just
  make sure you don't catch the sun in
  your shots as it is usually lower at this
  time of the day!; and

- Spend a lot of time making sure your
  colour grading is up to scratch as this
  will make the most difference in post
  production!

Day for Night shooting is a whole art onto
itself. I find it personally easier and more fun
just to go and shoot a scene in the night time.
However, feel free to try both methods and
find what works for you.

CHAPTER 04: SOUND

Sound

Do not neglect sound. There's the well known saying that sound is literally half of the movie. And I have to say, I agree. If you need convincing, try watching a horror movie without the sound. Spoiler: it won't be nearly even half as scary.

Bad sound is generally the number one indicator of an amateur filmmaker. It screams "I don't know what I'm doing!" If you have to choose between having poor visuals or poor sound, audiences will be far more forgiving of poor visuals - some will even believe that it is part of the directors vision and choice!

Now, there is a reason as to why all films have large, dedicated sound departments. Sound is complex and there is a lot to it. However, you can still get it right by using a small crew or even just shooting on your own.

The location

The location will have a huge impact on the sound quality, regardless of what hardware you use to record the sound. With the correct software and sound editing professional, you can normalise the sound from almost any location to make it sound sharp and professional - however, this requires a great amount of learning and skill. If you can avoid the unnecessary hassle, it is best to.

There are two main things you want to check while you are location scouting. Firstly, check for external noises which could prevent you from recording clean dialogue. Examples of this include noises from outside the location, such as if the location is based near a train station, you may end up having to deal with a noisy train every ten minutes or so. This could cause a significant disruption to your working day, if you have to pause every time the train is due to go past. There could also be noise from within the location which can prevent you from recording clean dialogue. An example of this is the humming sound from the refrigerator or air conditioning unit. An easy solution is of course just turning these electronic devices off, however make sure you have the owner's permission first.

The second thing to be mindful of when scouting a location is echo or reverberation. Part of this could be blocked by adding furniture into the room, if you are planning to do so. However, some areas are just too large and will always have an unwanted level of reverberation that you need to account for. Take it from someone who has learnt this the hard way, while reverberation is easy to add in post production, it is an absolute pain to take away. This is a problem that you are better off solving on location, rather than waiting until post production to try and fix.

One other point to consider when recording sound is that if you are shooting outdoors, you need to take wind levels into consideration. We have all seen amateur video recordings where there is a strong gust and the individual speaking on video is hard to hear or understand. Unless this is an artistic choice, this scenario should be avoided at all costs.

Thankfully, this is a problem which is easily solved. Whichever microphone you choose to use, if you are filming outdoors, you should try and use some kind of windshield - whether this is foam based, a dead cat or a wind shield. Either method will work, and will make your sound a million times more professional.

Equipment

While filmmakers often acknowledge the importance of sound, and agree that sound is half the movie going experience, they do not put their money where their mouth is when it comes to purchasing sound recording equipment. Most filmmakers spend most of their budget on a fancy camera and not nearly enough on good sound recording equipment.

I've noticed that a small minority of amateur filmmakers, especially those just starting out, are happy to use the microphone which is already built into their camera. I cannot stress enough how much this is not a good idea. In camera microphones are notorious for being awful, even amongst the more expensive DSLR or mirror-less cameras. Purchase an external microphone, there are a few different types which are recommended for filmmakers, which I will discuss below.

Of course the ideal situation is that you have a dedicated sound team. Whilst most of us cannot afford to pay sound professionals, we can still make do with an improvised version. The absolute best microphone for recording dialogue is a shotgun microphone. These are highly directional microphones which only pick up the sound in the direction of what they are pointed towards. This makes them ideal for a filmmaker as they will record high quality dialogue, whilst disregarding all other sounds which are not within its range or desired axis, such as someone humming in the background.

As shotgun microphones are incredibly directional, the microphone needs to be placed close to the subject's mouth in order to pick up dialogue clearly. This is why you often see dedicated boom operators on film sets, which are the individuals who are holding shotgun microphones on a boom pole, close to the subject's mouth. This clearly does not work for wide shots as you would be able to see the boom pole within the shot, however you can either choose to not record any dialogue through wide shots, or use a lavalier microphone, which is discussed in more detail below, for these types of shots.

Whilst you are unlikely to have a dedicated boom operator on your short film, there are two ways around this. Firstly, you can request that one of your actors, who is not on the screen at any given scene, operates the boom pole for you during that particular scene. Actors can rotate between scenes, and you can explain to your actors that as you do not have a dedicated sound professional on set, you wish for sound to be delegated as a more collective group effort, as there isn't a dedicated boom operator. If your actors are there throughout the day anyway, it is unlikely that they would mind helping out. The only problem with this method is that it assumes that all of your scenes will have at least one actor who is not on screen at that particular time which, if you are working on a short film with 1 to 3 actors, may not be likely.

An alternate method is purchasing a dedicated stand for your boom pole, and placing the stand and boom pole in position, out of shot, before you start recording and not moving the boom pole throughout the entire scene. This only works if there isn't much character or camera movement throughout the scene, which will work for some scenes and productions, but not for most.

An alternative system if you are shooting your film solo, as the only member of the crew is to use a lavalier microphone. These are often also referred to as tie-clip microphones, as they are small enough to be hidden under one's shirt. As lavalier microphones work at a very close range, they are incredibly good at picking up your actor's dialogue. In fact, it could be argued that they are too good as they often miss other noises, such as a dog barking in the distance or the natural reverberation of the room, which adds to the "realness" of the scene. Lavalier microphones are often wired, meaning both the microphone and the wire needs to be hidden, however there many inventive ways in which this can be done, the easiest of all being hidden under an actor's clothing.

Modern lavalier microphones work on a wireless basis, meaning they can be plugged directly into your camera and the audio and video is synced. This saves time in post production. The problem with this is that they wireless lavalier systems are generally on the more expensive side.

If you are looking for a lavalier system on a more budget friendly basis, I would recommend using a lavalier with an older portable recorder system. These are not wireless and therefore cannot be synced to the footage on your camera automatically which does create more work. However, if you buy these second hand, you can usually get them for a quarter of the price of the new, modern wireless systems.

If you opt to go for this system, you will need to manually synchronise the audio to your footage. However, this is not too difficult to get right. Firstly, buy a shotgun microphone to place on the top of your camera directly, to record sound directly to your footage. As the shotgun microphone is only recording reference sound which will not be actually used as the final sound in your short film, but is there just to refer to in order to match the sound from the lavalier microphone, you do

not need to buy an expensive, high quality
version. Instead, pick up a more affordable
option that fits your budget. You can also use
the in camera microphone if you really want
to, however, I personally like using a shotgun
microphone in the off chance that the audio
from your lavalier system does not work for
some reason or is corrupted, you still have the
dialogue recorded in a semi decent quality
which can still be used. As mentioned, since
this sound will not be particularly close to
your subjects, being placed directly on the
camera rather than close to your subjects, the
sound quality will not be immaculate. Instead,
use this sound during post production to gain
a reference point to replace it with the sound
recorded with the lavalier system. The easiest
way to synchronise the sound is to use a
clapper, which will give a spike in the noise,
which can then be used to match the two
audio systems. If you do not wish to purchase
a clapper, you can literally get your actors to
clap loudly right before they begin the scene,
which will produce a similar spike in the
audio wave, which can be synchronised
during post production.

As a general rule, you should always perform an audio test before you begin shooting to ensure all your systems are working correctly, your team know how to use the equipment and to troubleshoot any issues which arise even before you begin the actual shoot. You do not want to complete the shoot only to realise that the audio has not been recording correctly and you have just wasted all of your time. Always carry a pair of headphones with you to double check how the audio sounds from both your footage within the camera (recorded using the shotgun microphone) and on the portable recorder system which are using your lavalier microphone with.

Remember that things do go wrong from time to time. If you have a scene where the audio is out of sync, this doesn't mean that the particular scene in question is completely unusable. One way to overcome this is to send the footage to your actors and ask them to re-record the audio in time to the live scene playing out, so you can take the audio and place it over the scene, this is known as Automated Dialog Replacement, or ADR. If you have footage from various angles, you could show something else while the actors are speaking, so you cannot see their mouths and tell that the audio was recorded after the shoot had wrapped up.

Foley and sound effects

Foley is the recording of everyday sounds in post production, to be added to the film to make it appear more "natural". Examples of sounds which you may reproduce as foley are:

- Footsteps;
- The sound of clothes rustling as the character moves;
- Rustling of a newspaper;
- The sound of rain;
- A bone breaking etc.

There are tonnes of ways in which you can reproduce these sounds.

The most common sense way is, if possible, to recreate the action or movement and record it. An example of this is the sound of running on a pavement. You can just run and use a shotgun microphone to record the footsteps close to your feet.

However, it is not always possible to recreate the action you are trying to get a sound for. An example of this is if one of your character's breaks a bone. There are two ways around this. Firstly, the easy and less fun option is to look for the sound in an online foley database which may have the exact sound you are looking for, that you can just download and add to your production. The other option is to recreate the sound by being creative. There are plenty of examples of this online for different sounds. Let's say for example you want to recreate the sound of a bone breaking, you could try and snap some celery, which produces a similar sound, and then add this sound in post production to your scene.

A small distinction to be made is that foley often refers to more everyday sounds, whereas sound effects are larger than life, such as explosion. Sound effects can be recreated, but they can also be found online fairly easily and often gives a higher quality result that what you are able to recreate, due to their larger than life, high budget requirements.

CHAPTER 05: PROPS

Props

Film property, otherwise known as props, are any objects used by actors, or onscreen, during a film production. Props are movable objects, usually small in size, and do not include any fixtures or fittings, which are part of the location.

With film being a visual medium, props are important in telling a story. They can be used to set a scene, for example using an incorrect prop during a period or historical piece can completely take the audience out of the universe you have created. Let's take the example of Game of Thrones, whilst the audience will happily suspend its belief for dragons and necklaces which provide the illusion of youth, if Daenerys pulled out a smart phone during a scene and used it to call Jon Snow, it would completely ruin the audiences belief in the universe the show has created.

Similarly, good use of props can help alleviate your audience's perception of the universe you are creating. For example, if you are setting your short film in a 16th century upper class English dining room, using period piece cutlery can help add to the illusion that the characters are actually in that time period.

Good use of props can add to the audience's experience and should be considered very carefully when writing a script.

If you are attempting to make a zero budget short film, the best time to start considering what props you may need is when you begin planning and writing your script. You cannot afford to write a plot-driven script on a large scale military conflict, which requires realistic looking tanks, uniforms and weapons. Instead, you may decide to write a script on a soldier struggling to reintegrate into civilian life after serving in a conflict zone. It is best to stay away from historical pieces set in the past, as these require a lot of investment into props in order to create the correct setting.

If you do not have the money to buy props, the easiest way to get around this is to use what you already own. For example, if one of your hobbies involves sewing and you have a amazing, old school sewing machine, write a script where the main character is a tailor. Using items you already own has the added benefit of writing about what you know. In the previous example, if you do own a really awesome sewing machine, chances are that you know more than the average person about sewing and this knowledge should, in theory, help you when coming up with a story to tell. Not to say that you have to base your stories around your props, but you could use your props to add to the richness of the story. Perhaps your main character is dealing with poverty, and the sewing machine could be used as an aid to illustrate how he or she cannot afford to buy new clothes for her children, instead she repairs everything that they already own. The story isn't about sewing, but the prop in this instance is used to add to the idea that this character is living below the poverty line and adds an extra layer of detail to her life.

If you are in need of a specific prop, which you don't own, instead of rushing to the nearest market, sometimes it's easier just to ask around. You'll be amazed at what people will let you borrow, as long as you ask politely with a smile. Now I don't suggest asking strangers, people that don't know you don't owe you a thing, and are unlikely to be willing to lend to you. But ask within your circles, friends and family are a great place to start. You can even ask the people working on the film with you, such as the actors and any additional crew. After all, making a movie is a collaborative project, right? Just make sure that you always return the props back in the same condition that you borrowed them in! Don't be selfish and ask to borrow a prop, if you know the script requires you damaging it in some way.

If there really is a prop that you absolutely need for your project and you aren't able to borrow it from anywhere, then think about where you're going to buy it from. Buying second hand is almost always cheaper than buying new. Why not try and pick it up from a charity shop and do a good deed at the same time? Alternatively, there are plenty of bartering apps where people are happy to swap objects, rather than receiving cash for them. If there is something you are looking to get rid of, or have stopped using, but is still in god condition, why not help it find a new home? Otherwise, use sites like Gumtree, Craigslist or social media market places where people are trying to flock items they already own for a fraction of their retail price.

Remember that if you do buy a prop specifically for your project, you can use it more than once! For example, if you purchased a $20 item for one of your projects, you can help spread this cost out by making use of it in your other short films. You may decide to use it in additional 3 films, in which case, it has cost you $5 per short film. Don't force each prop you do end up buying into all your short films, but at the same time, if it can be utilised again, it makes sense to do so, at least from a financial point of view.

My last piece of advice on keeping the budget low when it comes to props is to use your imagination. What I mean by this is that sometimes it is much cheaper to create a D.I.Y. version of a prop, then to go out and actually

buy one. For example, if you need are making
a sci-fi movie set in a spaceship and need a set
of lights which are going to be used to focus
on the human hostage, it will be expensive
trying to find something futuristic. Instead,
you can grab a set of Christmas lights and
adapt these into various tubes or plastic
bottles that you can join together to create a
futuristic looking light set. Movies are all
about the illusion, you do not need to have the
real thing! Sure this might take a bit of work,
but try and enjoy the process of honing your
DIY skills. Consider the project as a mini art
piece, that is part of being a filmmaker, and
see how creative you can get.

CHAPTER 06: LOCATION

Location

Getting the ideal location(s) for your project can be costly and time consuming. The costs associated with hiring locations can be incredibly expensive, such as scouting for a location, ensuring it is safe and practical, creating changes at the location to make it suit the needs of the story, paying the day rate needed to secure the location and returning it back to its normal condition all cost a lot of money. Of course it's important to get the locations right for your story. A story revolving around an elderly couple from the countryside obviously can't be shot in the middle of Times Square. A good location can add to the texture of the visual medium and as a filmmaker it is your duty to consider the impact of the location of the overall story and visuals of the film.

The ideal situation would probably be getting access to a film studio, where you can either shoot against a green screen, if you are working within the sci-fi genre, or creating the exact set that you envisioned when writing the script. This way you can decide each and every aspect of the "location" as it is your own artificial creation that you have full control over.

However, this is clearly not an option for someone on a zero budget project, unless you already have strong contacts with someone who owns a film studio. Therefore, we will settle on filming in real locations. Even if the location you find is not perfect, you are always able to make amendments, such as moving, adding or removing furniture as necessary. As a general rule of thumb, just ensure the room has the right feel to it and it you are practically able to shoot there, without too many logistical problems. Redesigning the set, or only using certain camera angles to capture parts of the location and exclude other parts, can solve most other minor visual issues.

One of the easiest and most simple ways to keep the costs down when it comes to locations is to choose to shoot in as few locations as possible. Part of the reason why Martin Scorsese's The Irishman was so expensive was due to the fact that it was shot at 117 different locations. Think about all the location related costs it incurred, which I mentioned in the first paragraph of this chapter, and the costs of moving all the cast and crew to each of these locations. Ideally, if you are able to get your short film down to a single location, you are onto a winner. Now, I know what you're thinking, reducing the number of locations will take away from your story. Well, not necessarily. Firstly, there are many full length feature films which are shot in a single location, such as Rodrigo Cortès' Buried, starring Ryan Reynolds, or Steven Knight's Locke, starring Tom Hardy. And full length feature films are more difficult to shoot in a single location due to needing to keep the audience captivated over a long period of time. Which brings me onto my second point, it is much easier shooting a *short* film in a single location, than it would be shooting a full feature length movie. This is due to the reduction in time allowed to tell the story,

which results in stories needing to be simpler.
Many directors have shot award winning
short films in a single location, and captured
the audiences imagination throughout. You
just need to be creative and you will find
yourself turning this limitation into a strength.
In fact part of the reason why Buried was so
engaging was that it was only shot in a single
location! Chris Sparling, the writer of Buried,
used the idea of the main character being
trapped in a single location as the main selling
point of the story.

The obvious answer to keeping the costs as
low as possible is to pick a location(s) which is
easily accessible to you, which you will not
need to pay for. Now, we can split this into
two separate categories.

The first category is shooting within an indoor
location. If you are planning on getting a free
location, this will most likely be your home.
Regardless of whether you own your place,
are renting or live in your parent's house, this
is a great starting point for shooting short
films as it is not only free but is accessible
throughout the day giving you more flexibility
regarding when you are able to shoot your

film. Set your short film in your apartment, perhaps creating a drama based around family dynamics, a horror story where the main character is trapped in his/her room etc.

The second category involves shooting in an outside environment. This can literally be most places which are dedicated spaces for the public, for example a park or a local forest. Avoid areas which are heavily populated with businesses as this can lead to friction over shooting on private property which is owned by someone else, having logos in the background etc. Ideally shoot in a location where there will be little interruptions from other people in order to have an efficient shooting day. People are often curious when they see a camera and some actors. This can lead to constant questioning from the public which can add up when you are on a tight schedule. Always be polite in order to avoid any potential conflicts, however learn to be firm with people and explain that you are on a tight schedule and therefore cannot indulge in a longer conversation. If you do choose to shoot in a busy public area, such as near a shopping centre, because of what the story demands, then try and work in these areas during quieter times, such as early on a Sunday morning, or during antisocial hours like 5am or 6am in the morning on a weekend. This way you will have access to the location, with minimal interruptions.

If you have any friends, family or even actors or crew members that you have worked with before who have access to some amazing locations, don't be afraid to ask if you can shoot there over a few hours! This works especially well if you help communicate your vision and why having that particular location will help you achieve it. Be polite and offer to send them the final product and make them feel involved in the process. If the person takes an interest in your career or the project, they are more likely to not only help you out in this one instance, but potentially repeatedly in the future as well.

One huge potential downfall in exterior location hunting, depending on your local and national legal system, can be obtaining filming permits. This can be very time consuming, not to mention an additional expense which most amateur filmmakers cannot afford to pay. It is something worth looking up before choosing an exterior location and deciding whether the cost is justifiable. There have been many examples of filmmakers shooting "guerrilla style" without permits, such as James Cameron did infamously during the shooting of the original Terminator movies, whether this is the correct route for you can only be a personal decision, however I would always recommend staying on the right side of the law.

Working with businesses

As mentioned earlier, aim to steer clear of businesses as this can lead to issues further down the line. If the short film gains a lot of traction and the company believes you have not asked permission to film, this can result in a messy and costly situation. But what if you need to shoot in a business, such as a grocery store? The main approach I would recommend in this scenario can be summarised as follows: you don't ask, you don't get. Although, what you're thinking is probably true: most businesses will say no. Why wouldn't they? What have you got to offer? And that's the approach you should take. Speak to the business owner and explain how the situation will be mutually beneficial for both parties. On the one hand, you have a place to film. Meanwhile, you can agree to show the business' logo and maybe mention the location or city where they are based in your dialogue. This is essentially free marketing for the business, something that most companies love. Bear in mind that this will probably not work with huge corporations as most people are already aware of their business, so it might be more worthwhile targeting local up and coming businesses instead. Also, you can explain how you are planning to do a mini "press run" in your local area, such as interviews with local newspapers and radio stations, and if they agree to let you film with them, you will plug their company at each of these events. Again, this is positive marketing for the company as they are seen as working with local talent and helping the community where they can.

Location Scouting

The saying time is money also applies in regards to which location you choose for your project. Extra time spent at the location can mean additional costs incurred in many forms, from direct extra costs in paying for the location as you may have to spend extra time there, to additional indirect costs, such as your shooting time being longer due to issues encountered with the location, resulting in extra pay for staff, prop and equipment rental etc. Therefore one of the best pieces of advice when filming in a new location is to actual visit the location beforehand. It is never a good idea to just rock up on the day and hope for the best - neither from a financial, nor creative point of view. When visiting a location beforehand, I do not mean having a quick five minute look around, but actually spending a few hours scouting a location and making sure it is the correct fit. Things to look out for include:

- Ensuring the location matches the theme and aesthetic you are looking to reflect in your story. For example, a story set in the 1920's can't be shot easily in a modern open-plan house.

- Have a look at the lighting. Depending on which way the windows are facing may dictate which rooms will be best to film in during certain parts of the day to get the most out of the natural sunlight. Planning your shots in this fashion can lead to an aesthetically superior film. There are plenty of apps which you can download which tell you which direction sunlight is coming in from and which direction it will move throughout the day. Use this to inform which rooms you are better off working in during the morning vs. the afternoon.

- Have a look at the layout of the space which can dictate what type of shots you are able to get. If you are planning to shoot in a tight corridor, this may limit the size of your lighting equipment and you may have to rely on more of a handheld style of shooting. It is a lot easier trying to plan your shots and equipment in advance when you are familiar with the space.

- Spend some time at the location to learn about any audio issues. Listen out for cars, trains or planes which regularly pass by. Are they loud enough to interrupt your audio? Is there a fridge, air conditioning unit or other mechanical device which continually makes loud noises which you may have to account for? Again, planning is key here.

- Lastly, have a look at any practical issues you may face. For example, are there enough power sockets for all the electrical equipment you intend to use or are you going to have to bring an extension lead?

Home studio

The very last tip on getting a free or next to free location is the use of film studios. As mentioned earlier, hiring a film studio is out of the question for most people starting out. However, if you are a homeowner or are renting a larger place and have a spare room, create your own! This doesn't have to be expensive. Have a blank room which you can adapt and base your scripts off this potential space. This option will not, of course, be available to everyone, but for those of you lucky enough to be in this position - use it!

CHAPTER 07: THE SCRIPT

The Script

A script is the heart of your short film. It is the body of your film, with directional choices adding a personality and soul. A common joke amongst screenwriters is that being a screenwriter is like being that kid in school who tells a funny joke to his friend, and his friend then retells the joke to the entire class and makes them all laugh, with the friend being the director in this scenario. This joke is crudely suggesting that screenwriters come up with the content, and it is the director's role to nail the delivery and bring it to life.

Do I even need a script?

While it is true that some directors choose not to use scripts at all, this is a minority and only works for certain types of people and productions. Some directors prefer to have a rough idea of what they wish to achieve, arrive on set with their actor(s) and crew, and improvise the entire production. As mentioned, this may work for a certain personality type, who does not like to plan and prefers to make impulsive decisions. Alternatively, directors who have a strong connection with their actors and crew, if they have worked with them previously, may be confident that they can produce an interesting short film with just an idea. This is usually experienced directors who can work without a set script and story board. Moreover, the idea behind your movie may dictate whether you need a script. As an example, if you are producing a "day in the life" type movie, such as those created by Richard Linklater, over a period of time, you may prefer to improvise continuously to get more of an authentic change in plot, rather than working based on a rigid and pre-determined guideline. Although a good script will allow movement for improvisation and minor changes, which is something that you may choose to do on the day, or your actors may wish to improvise.

As someone starting out, whilst of course you are free to try this method, it is not recommended as there is a lot to control, without a schedule. It is all too easy to forget to shoot a scene, or coverage from a specific angle or even overlook a plot hole which weakens the entire story. A script can help dictate pace, story, direction and avoid standing around with actors and crew with nothing to do.

To write or not to write? That is the question.

There is always the assumption within the amateur filmmaking community that all up and coming filmmakers will naturally take on the role of both writer and director, and will write the script that they will later direct. Whilst, this is the case with many directors who have risen to fame, such as Quentin Tarantino, Christopher Nolan, Paul Thomas Anderson etc., the majority of directors actually stick mainly to directing. This is not to say that they do not make adjustments to the script that they initially receive, in fact many directors make enough changes to warrant a writing credit on the film. However, it is typical in Hollywood for a director to receive a script from a writer and bring the film to life from there. Many talented directors know their limits and when to outsource, which is part of what makes them so talented. You can still be an amazing director whilst adapting a script someone else has written. Some of the most iconic films of all time are as a result of a director collaborating with a dedicated screenwriter, examples of which include Taxi Driver (directed by Martin Scorsese and written by Paul Schrader), Psycho (directed by Alfred Hitchcock and written by Joseph Stefano) and Schindler's List (directed by Steven Spielberg and written by Steven Zaillian). Although this is fairly accepted in the mainstream film industry, there is no shame pursuing this route as an amateur filmmaker, if you know that your neither your talents or interest lie in script writing.

So how do you go about getting your hands on a script as an amateur filmmaker who hasn't made a name for themselves yet? Well, the obvious answer is to buy a script. There are tonnes of screenwriting forums where individuals post their scripts for sale. It may take a lot of time going through various scripts finding one which resonates with you. Do not expect to find the next Hollywood blockbuster on these forums, these are amateur screenwriters looking to share their work and hone their craft, therefore expect there to be adjustments which need to be made. The other difficulty with getting a readymade script is that, as you are on a budget, a lot of the stories may require certain aspects, such as props or locations, which are out of your budget. If you are expecting to purchase a script, do not forget to haggle the price down. You are not buying a professional feature length script, but rather an amateur short film script, so do not expect to pay much, especially if the screenwriter does not have a strong history of getting their scripts made into successful productions.

The other option, if you not a writer yourself, is to collaborate with other writers in order to get a script. The big advantage of this, as opposed to purchasing an already finished script, is getting to tailor the script to a story which suits you. As you are likely to be limited in resources, you can commission a screenwriter to write a script with a set number of actors, limited to certain location(s) and using only certain props etc. which allows you to meet your monetary criteria. There are many screenwriters, who just like directors, are wanting to get their foot in the door and recognise their talents or interest can only be limited to one aspect of filmmaking, in this case being writing. They may be more than happy to provide you a script for free, in exchange for credit on their resume and experience of getting one of their scripts made into an actual production.

By collaborating, you are making the most of both of your talents. Whilst you can simply ask the writer to write your script and fly off the handle from here, it is sometimes best to truly collaborate and continue to involve the writer in further decisions or changes you wish to make. This is because the writer should know the script inside out and can help inform you if the changes you are making will have an effect on certain characters or plotlines later in the script. They may also offer a different perspective to the one you have considered which could make the film even better than what you had planned.

You can find a writer either online or locally. The big advantage to finding a writer locally is the collaboration aspect I have just mentioned. They may even be able to come along to

rehearsals to the actual shoot and provide
further input. This is also a great way to find a
career-long collaborator, which is great if your
styles complement each other. The other
alternative is finding a collaborator through
the internet. While you may lose the local
touch, you will have a wider range of writers
to choose from and therefore can find
someone's writing style which sparks your
interest.

The Writer Director

On the other hand, there are many filmmakers
who couldn't imagine separating the art of
writing and director from a single role. These
individuals have a burning desire to tell a
story and wish to have control of the
production from its inception to the final cut.

If you are a new filmmaker who doesn't know
whether or not they are going to be good at or
enjoy the writing process - there is no harm in
giving it a go. Remember that writing is a
learned skill, so you are unlikely to produce an
incredible script on your first attempt. You
will likely have to write many scripts before
settling on one which you are happy to shoot.

Even when you do find an engaging story which you have a desire to bring to life, the script will likely have many rewrites and drafts. This is true for professionals and will most likely be true for you too.

One thing to bear in mind is that short scripts require a different writing style to feature length scripts. With the film being shorter in length, this obviously provides some limitations, which if you are creative, can be turned into strengths. For example, there is less time to get to know each character and therefore less time for the audience to familiarise themselves with your characters and empathise with them. One way around this is to use less characters, which means the audience has a better chance on focusing on them. For instance, you're more likely to get your audience to invest in two characters in a 5 minute short film than 20 characters. There is also less time, which means the plot cannot be as elaborate. Great, this is an opportunity to jump right into the action without a back story and expose your audience to the most exciting part of your character's journey. There are many free online resources which delve into what makes a great short script. Use these as a starting point, however, trial and error is the best teacher when it comes to developing your own unique voice as a filmmaker. In a certain sense, you do not want to be following what everyone else is doing in the industry. However, it is worth learning the rules, before breaking them. That way you can pick and choose which rules to break and which to stick to, in order to create the best structure for your story.

Software

Speaking of utilising free online resources, you will need specialist writing software in which to write your script. Of course you can just a standard word processing software, however industry standard scripts have so many formatting rules that this will take you forever and a day to get right. But why do I need to write to industry standards if I'm just producing a short film? Good question. Well, part of the reason for producing short films is to prepare yourself for larger feature films, for most people. If this is not your intention, feel free to ignore my advice. Eventually when you start working with professionals, they will expect industry standard formatting. In fact, you could end up ruining an opportunity if asked to present a script as you may be seen as an amateur hobbyist, rather than a professional. It is better to get into good habits straight away. There are many online screenwriting software websites which allow you to use their services, or a basic version of their more advanced services, for free. At the stage of your career you are currently operating at, these should be sufficient to meet your needs.

Working to a budget

When writing the script, you can tailor certain elements of the script to ensure that you are keeping production costs to a minimum. These are discussed in more detail throughout the book, however a brief summary is as follows:

- Number of characters: the larger the number of characters, the more complex the production will be. This may result in increased costs such as actor fees, catering, number of crew required to work and their fees, equipment needed etc. Therefore, it is

best to minimise the number of
characters within your short film.

- Location: The first thing to consider is
  the number of locations. The more
  locations, the more cost will be incurred
  in paying for the locations, as well as
  paying for your actors and crew to
  move between locations. The second
  thing to consider is which locations are
  available to you. If you base your script
  around locations which you have free
  access to, this will reduce the overall
  cost of your production.

- Action sequences: This may seem like a
  strange thing to mention, but action
  sequences can be very costly. If you are
  aiming for an ambitious action
  sequence, such as an intense fight scene,
  it is imperative that you use a stunt
  team and get insurance. It is not worth
  trying to save money when there is the
  potential for individuals to get injured
  on your set. Safety trumps all else. Be
  realistic with your action sequences, it
  is unlikely you will have the gear to
  carry out a car chase. So write in a foot

chase instead. If shot correctly, this can be just as exciting.

- The context: What I mean by this is the setting in which the story takes place. Whether this is in modern times, or set in the 1600's in rural Japan or whether it is set 200 years in the future in an alternate universe. This will inform a lot of your filming decisions which can cost money. Generally, the rule is that the further away from your current situation the story is set, the more expensive it will be to recreate it. Of course there are huge exceptions to the rule and it depends on how crafty and imaginative you are as a filmmaker. But nonetheless, it is a good starting point. Let's say your story is set 200 years in the future in an alternate universe, this will affect decisions such as lighting (in order to create a futuristic effect), wardrobe (as your characters will almost certainly dress differently) and the props you need (you may have to make some of these, as the story is set in an alternate universe). This is not to say do not deviate from shooting with

what is available to you, but plan for
the differences to keep the costs low.

Plot-based vs. Character-based stories

You may also have to consider your
limitations as a filmmaker on a budget when
writing the script, in terms of the type of story
you are able to tell. In filmmaking, there are,
broadly speaking, two types of films: plot
based and character based. Plot based films
are those which require action to move the
story forward. An example of this may be a
heist film, like Steven Soderbergh's Ocean's
Eleven, where the actions of the characters are
used to move the story in different directions.
These scripts tend to involve many characters,
over many locations. The alternative to this is
a character based movie, which tends to
revolve around an individual or a small group
of people and their behaviours and feelings
tend to move the story in different directions.
A great example of this is Steven Knight's
Locke, where the movie revolves around a
single character in a car. Of course these two
categories are not mutually exclusive, nor are
the characteristics of each movie exclusive.
You can have character based films shot in

many locations with a very high budget, like Todd Philip's Joker. However, as a amateur filmmaker on a budget, you will be leaning more towards a character based film.

The heart of these movies is the relationship between characters and the way they feel about themselves. This is often revealed in dialogue. It is *crucial* that you learn how to write good dialogue as a filmmaker. This will make or break your short film. One of the best ways to learn how to write good dialogue is to watch films and read scripts from directors whose style you admire. Alternatively, if you want your films to be grounded in reality, you can take inspiration from real life people you know or genuine conversations you have had or observed.

The only hard and fast rule is to keep it interesting. Aside from this, be as creative as you dare.

The last recommendation I would have is to keep the script efficient. As a general rule, one page of your screenplay is equivalent to one minute of screen time. Of course this is dependent on the amount of dialogue, action sequences etc. but it is generally used in the industry as a rough basis. Therefore, there are two ways in which you can approach a script. Firstly, you can be incredibly efficient and only keep key scenes in the screenplay, which you intend to shoot. An example of this is Christopher Nolan's debut feature film, Following, which was just under 90 pages long. Everything that was written was shot and subsequently used in the film. This is because Nolan was shooting on expensive 16mm stock film, and in order to keep the cost down, Nolan did not keep anything in the script that he was not intending to shoot. Compare this to the Bollywood blockbuster, Lagaan, directed by Ashutosh Gowariker, where the first cut of the film was a staggering 7 and a half hours. As an amateur filmmaker, it is important to find the balance. I would not recommend making a script so efficient that you have no room to add or remove scenes in post-production, this will provide you with less artistic choice. Alternatively, do not create such a long script that you have hours of spare footage which you know you will have to disregard. Aim to be efficient, but with flexibility, an extra scene or two isn't going to add tonnes of cost and time to your production, but it may make the difference between a good and great film in the editing room.

CHAPTER 08: HIRING ACTORS

Hiring Actors

We often hear the stories about the incredible amounts that Hollywood studios pay some of their actors. I remember reading a little while ago about how Robert Downey Jr. was paid circa $75 million for his role in Avengers: Infinity War, as well as the same amount in Avengers: Endgame. As to the accuracy of these figures, I cannot vouch for them, but it is not unreasonable for an actor of Robert Downey Jr.'s calibre to receive such an amount. It got me thinking about why actors are able to command such large amounts for their parts in movies. Of course, there is an element of marketability within this. There will be fans who will go to the theatre because they are fans of Robert Downey Jr., meaning he is an attraction for fans to see the movie in the first place. However, there is more to it than just that: a good actor can be the difference between a great movie or an awful one. Audiences care heavily about an actor's performance and it is a key element to creating the illusion and bringing the audience into the fictional world you are trying to create as a filmmaker.

Casting the right actor(s) is crucial to the success of your short film and time should not be spared when trying to find the right actor.

The Hiring Process

The temptation when looking for actors on a budget is to immediately turn to friends and family as they be more than willing to work for free to help you out. However, given the importance of hiring the right actors as we have just discussed above, unless your family and friends are experienced actors, this may not be the best route to go down. Even if your friends and family are experienced actors, it is still not always the best idea to work with people you are incredibly close to as it may be difficult to be objective when judging their performance, or you may be hesitant to criticise their performances in fear of hurting their feelings and jeopardising your personal relationship. This isn't to say that you shouldn't work with friends and family, just consider the points above before doing so.

Hiring inexperienced actors will create more problems and result in a far more amateur production which can only harm your end product. Nothing screams student film or inexperienced filmmaker like bad acting, it is characteristic of student films to hire their friends in roles in which they are unqualified to play, like seeing a student trying to play his friends dad even though they are the same age. It just doesn't work. Therefore, I would recommend hiring actors with some film experience, even if this is just working on amateur plays or on other director's short films. As an inexperienced director yourself, trying to get a good performance out of completely inexperienced actors may be too much of a challenge. Getting good performances out of actors is a skill in itself, which requires a lot of practice. This is something which you will learn and eventually be good at, however just starting out, it will be best for your own development to take baby steps and hire actors who already know what they're doing and just need creative guidance rather than technical guidance as well. It may also help you learn about the filmmaking process if you are working with experienced actors, as they may be able to share their previous positive and negative experiences with you, which you could incorporate into your own productions.

The first step to hiring actors is to put up an advertisement which announces that you are looking for actors for your short film, with details of the film and the role. Luckily, there are plenty of advertising methods which are free or there are free versions available. Examples of which include listing the advert with local theatre companies, posting on social media or posting on casting websites. The latter method is my preferred choice as you have the largest volume of actors available all in one space. However, more local methods such as placing an advert with a local theatre company may be preferable if you are racing against a tight deadline. The best advice at this stage is to make sure the advert is detailed. I would include details such as:

- providing a brief description of the story;

- detailing any physical characteristics that you require within the character;

- going into detail about the characters personality; and

- practical points such as potential shooting dates, number of shooting days, size of the production, level of pay (if any), whether expenses will be reimbursed, audition dates etc.

Usually, on these casting websites, there is a lot of interest from candidates. However, often many actors apply to any and every job they can in the hope of gaining some work, or gaining some versatility on their resume. It is your job to ensure that they are the right fit for the role. As a starting point, eliminate anybody who is clearly not a physical match for the role, for example anyone who doesn't fit into the right age bracket. Next, it is often clear, from the personalised messages often sent with the application whether they have taken any time in reading your story or whether this is part of a saying "yes" to everything campaign. Only hire people who took the time to read your description, these are the hard workers who are serious about their craft.

Even if the actors believe they may be right for their role, it is your role to assess whether they actually are. Usually, this is done by a casting director. However, based on the limited budget, you can easily do this role yourself. Besides, this will help you get a feel of the actor's raw talent from the very beginning, making it easier to adapt your style of directing in order to get the best performance out of them.

Another temptation that arises when auditioning actors on a budget is to simply request a video audition which they can send to you and selecting your actors based off this. This is a great starting point as you can get a feel of what the actor's interpretation of your character is, whether they are on the same page as you in terms of character interpretation and whether they possess the level and type of charisma you need for your character.

Of course it is a good idea to look at their video reels from their previous work, if they have one, but this will not necessarily inform you on how they interpret the character you have written. From the video auditions, you should aim to shortlist no more than 10 candidates which you can actually see playing your role. Remember that not all of them would have interpreted the role in the same way you did when you wrote it, this is not necessarily a bad thing. Sometimes it is worth exploring different options as they may be able to add a different dimension to your character which you failed to notice.
Actors are often very good at understanding the depths of a character and a good actor should be able to unveil parts of a character which you haven't fully been able to explore.

Once you have shortlisted your actors, you should audition them whilst you are in the same space. There are two ways to go about this: either invite them to see you or go and visit them. The latter option can end up being very costly as it requires a lot of personal travelling for yourself. However if you are in a city with cheap public transport or already have a car and the actors are all fairly close, this could work out cheaper than hiring out a room. The other, and most common, option is to get the actors to come to you. This way you can audition all the actors back to back in a single day, saving time and money. As mentioned earlier, if you are upfront about when the auditions will be held during your initial advert, this will reduce the likelihood of people dropping out. In order to keep the cost as low as possible, the best possible scenario is using a space for the auditions which you can access for free. It is not unreasonable to hold the auditions in your living room. If you have no space available where you can audition, then the space you hire essentially needs to be an empty room, it should not matter if it is devoid of character. Find the cheapest space you can find for a single or half day, depending on the number of actors you wish to audition, and hire this out.

Aim to fix a single date for the auditions as multiple dates means hiring out a space for longer period. This is why I recommended short listing only 10 actors or less, per role. Often, the approach casting directors take is to audition hundreds of actors on a single day, and then re-auditioning their favourites on a single day. This is obviously more costly as you need to hire out an audition room for multiple days, as well as organising transport to get there over multiple days. Plus, in my opinion, this is overkill for a short film. A short film should be a relatively short commitment, therefore look for the best fit for your role, but it is not necessary to find the perfect fit. The way to ensure that you get a good fit through a single day of auditions is to spend longer with each actor and making sure they are both a good actor and a good fit in terms of the right personality to ensure a good working relationship for you and the culture you are trying to create on set.

You should provide the actor's with the same monologue/dialogue from your short film, which will allow you to assess how they respond to your script. Moreover, by forcing all the actors to audition the same segment of your script, this allows you to make comparisons easier between characters. If the actors all auditioned using any monologue they preferred, this makes it different to compare performances, especially if the chosen scenes demonstrate a range of emotions. As a general rule, I find it best to let the actors audition raw for the first take to get their interpretation and then guiding them and making suggestions for a few additional takes to understand how they respond to your directorial technique. Almost use the day as a mini rehearsal day, as well as an audition day to get the right fit.

Just because you are conducting the auditions over a single day, does not mean that you have to decide who you want on the same day. In fact, I would recommend waiting at least two to three days before approaching the decision with a fresh mind. It is easy to get caught up in who you liked the most as a person and offering them the role, however this does not necessarily mean they are the right fit for the role.

There are plenty of examples of Hollywood actors being difficult to work with, despite churning out fantastic performances. Different people have different ways of working. As long as they are not disrespectful to you or other colleagues, sometimes you have to put up with eccentric behaviour in order to get a great performance. If you are serious about directing, don't let this put you off, instead learn to work with it. One way which I have used to help maintain objectivity when choosing actors is to film the auditions. This way I can come back to the performance a few days later and approach it with a fresh pair of eyes. This also has two additional benefits: firstly, you are able to pick up on small nuances which you may have missed before which will add to the performance and secondly you can determine which actors are favoured by the camera. Some actors will work great for live performances, such as auditions, but as Sidney Lumet explains, they will just not be loved by the camera.

The Production Process

The most obvious and largest cost associated with actors will be their fee. This can also be the largest expense on most amateur film sets. As you are working with amateur film actors, of course the fee will not be too high. However, have a look at what the average day rate is for actors around your local area, this is what you should be able to negotiate. However, for most short films, actors are usually not paid. The morality of this is

definitely debatable, however the logic behind
it is that it is an unpaid project for all parties
involved for which nobody will earn any
money. It is used as a learning experience for
all parties. As a general rule, you should offer
the actors full access to the short film which
they are able to use in their show reels, which
can help them land paid roles. Most actors
which audition for short films are usually
either students or at the beginning of their
careers, so this is something to bear in mind
when directing.

However, the downside to requesting actors to
work for free is that there is no commitment to
you. If they are offered a paid role or even a
more interesting role from elsewhere, they are
likely to take that up instead. It is not entirely
uncommon for actors not to show up on the
planned days of shooting, sometimes even
without having informed you at all. This can
be incredibly frustrating, especially when you
have paid out for other things such as the
venue, or there are multiple actors and you are
unable to proceed if one of your actors decides
to bail, effectively meaning you are unable to
proceed with the production at all. Therefore,
if you are paying out costs and are relying

actors to turn up, paying them for their time almost guarantees that they will turn up. If you are paying your actors, you can also draw up a contract, which will almost guarantee they will show up to the production. And if they do not, you can claim breach of contract, and thus recover your funds through a small court.

Always check what your local and national laws say in regards to unpaid work. Being an employer is a big responsibility, don't cut corners or operate outside the law. It is never worth the risk. Often, most actors will operate as self employed and hence you do not need to worry about employer taxes etc. But nonetheless, always check first.

It is also worth looking up whether your actors have signed up with a union as they may have minimum amounts they are allowed to work for. For example, some unions force their members to charge a minimum daily rate for their experience level. It does not take long to ask your actors whether they are part of a union and look up the relevant rules. It is also worth checking with most unions as they have a helpline. Often, the onus is on the members to comply with the rules so don't worry too much, however it is never a good idea to get on the wrong side of a union, this could have long term negative effects, especially as you become more senior in the industry.

A great pro tip is to schedule your shoots effectively based on actors' availability. If you minimise the time you need to initially shoot your film and need actors on set for, as well as reducing the chances of a retake (by ensuring you get multiple shots and extra footage during initial production), this should save on costs. Even if you are collaborating with actors who are generously offering their time up for free, you may have other costs such as location costs which will be reduced as a result of this efficiency.

CHAPTER 09: WARDROBE

Wardrobe

Wardrobe decisions help the audience to believe the illusion that the characters are living within a particular context and can be critical to allowing the audience to believe the illusion. A significant chunk of a blockbuster movie's production is spent on wardrobe for both the actors and extras. This includes clothes, but also can include accessories such as jewellery pieces. However, if you watch most amateur short films, wardrobe rarely plays a large part in the illusion of the movie. Therefore, it is strongly worth considering, as a starting point, whether wardrobe decisions are even important within your script and worth spending time and money on. If the film is set within the modern world, amongst characters with 'everyday' backgrounds, then the actors should be able to wear their every

day clothes without taking anything away
from the script.

Of course this depends on the subject matter
of your script and the context within which is
set. Factors which affect wardrobe include, but
are not limited to:

- the time period your story is set in e.g.
  characters from 500 years ago will be
  expected to dress much differently to
  modern day characters;

- the class the characters are operating in
  e.g. if you are remaking a story like
  Wuthering Heights, Heathcliff would
  be expected to dress very differently
  from when he was 'lower' class to when
  he became 'upper' class;

- the age that the characters are playing;
  and

- the culture that the characters come
  from, which can include their ethnic
  background.

Therefore, in order to minimise wardrobe costs, all of the above needs to be considered when writing your script. That is not to say that every single script that you write should be set in the modern day, within the country you are based in and circumstances you are living in. However, they need to be considered as to whether they are realistic.

If the film is set in modern times, then the easiest option is going to be to ask the actors to bring their own clothes, or even just acting in whatever they decide to wear that day, if the wardrobe isn't particularly important. Alternatively, if you are aiming for a specific look, then don't be afraid to either lend them your clothes or ask around with friends or family to see what will fit and what you can make use of. It is worth even asking the actors whether they own the clothes you are looking to include in your short film. You never know what their personal style is, or whether they have acted in a production set in the same context beforehand which they happen to still own the wardrobe pieces for. It is always worth asking, the worst case scenario is that you make no progress and end up in exactly the same position you were already in.

If the wardrobe requirements are fairly
unusual, such as a costume for a peasant in
medieval times, it may be worth dropping by
your local theatre company or film school and
asking if they have anything which would
meet your requirements. Explain what you are
trying to achieve and why, often you will be
asked to pay a refundable deposit and most
companies will be happy to help you out if
they are able to. They will have access to
costumes which they have acquired for
various productions throughout their time
which they might not be using, that they
would rather be used than just collect dust.
Even if you have to pay a small fee for hiring
out the costumes, this will still be far cheaper
than purchasing a new wardrobe or having it
made from scratch. Don't forget to offer to
show your finished film, as a thank you. This
also has the added benefit of potentially
making some fantastic connections with other
people working in the same industry.

If none of the above options fit your criteria
and you are forced to buy clothes, then your
first port of call should always be trying to buy
clothes second hand. Good places to look are

car boot sales, online retailers like Ebay or
Amazon, social media market places etc. With
second hand clothing, you can get the same
costumes for a fraction of the price. As the old
saying goes: "one man's trash is another man's
treasure."

Of course this only works if the costume isn't
wildly specific, such as a period piece. These
types of costumes tend to be incredibly
expensive, as they are essentially one-off
costumes which need to be tailor made. If you
are working on a large scale Hollywood
production, this is what the dedicated
wardrobe department will hand make for you,
to your exact specification. However, for a
short film on a budget, you may have to get
creative. Instead of aiming for a completely
finished end product, perhaps just get a piece
of clothing which somewhat resembles what
you are trying to achieve and then adjusting it
to fit your needs. This may require
accessorising it, or even getting the old sewing
machine out to make some changes.

Don't forget to consider colours in your
wardrobe design. Film is a visual medium and
colours are an easy way or getting the

audience to subconsciously relate a certain emotion to your scene. Consider wardrobe to be part of the larger colour scheme of your set and film. For example, during Steven Spielberg's Jaws, the colour yellow was always used somewhere on screen to indicate danger. If we take a similar concept and apply it to the wardrobe decisions in your short film, a dark colour like grey can be used to indicate the character's bland mood at the start of the film. The final scene of the film could involve the same character wearing a mostly bright red colour to indicate love and happiness being bought into her life. Wardrobe choices are a great, subtle way to convey emotions throughout your scene and their importance should be considered in the context of the film's theme, rather than as an ad-hoc decision to just make your actors look pretty.

One final point to bear in mind is that audiences will be more forgiving knowing you are a low budget amateur filmmaker, than if you were making a Hollywood blockbuster. Keep this in mind and don't necessarily aim for perfection. As long as it is not bad enough to break the illusion, there are other factors which you can rely on to create the reality and immerse your audience, such as the acting, the setting, props etc. It is only one part of a much larger equation.

CHAPTER 10: CREW

Crew

Having a crew involves hiring team members, and particularly those with experience, which can end up being costly. As a an amateur filmmaker on a budget, I often look as having a crew to be a luxury, rather than a necessity to most of my short films. Don't get me wrong, having a crew on certain productions is essential, as you physically won't have enough hands to get everything done. But more often than not, with the smaller productions (i.e. the ones I'm working on which have literally next to no budget), having a crew would save a lot of headache, but I can often do their role. The key is to swap out their expertise for your time. Sure, they may be able to do in half an hour what it takes you two hours to do, but this is part of the compromise of being an amateur filmmaker, on a budget.

And as someone who wants to keep costs as low as possible, I would recommend doing as much as you possibly can on your own. This does have the disadvantage of being far more time consuming and bearing a lot more pressure on yourself as you have less people to rely on. However, as an amateur filmmaker, you aren't set to a strict timeline as your films are most likely to be self funded. It does also mean that your film cannot be scaled to be as large as other productions, however if you are producing short films for next to nothing, compromises have to be made.

If you have friends or family who have an interest in filmmaking and are willing to help out, by all means take them up on their offer. Even a single extra crew member can ease the workload significantly. However, going forwards, I will assume that this isn't a luxury that most of you will have.

There are also advantages to trying to take on as many of the crew's roles as you can by yourself. The main advantage, outside of it being much cheaper, is that you can gain an understanding of what each role required. This means that when you are ready to move onto productions with a crew, you will have an understanding of their role and therefore be better able to direct them, and explain what you need.

Below I have listed the larger crew roles, usually found in feature films. The vast majority of short films would not even dream of having a crew this extensive. The reason why I've listed out the roles is for you to think about how you can perform their role on your short film. While the list may seem long and overwhelming at first, as your short film is on a much smaller scale than a large, Hollywood blockbuster - some of the roles can be minimised to a few, simple decisions at the pre-production stage.

Director

A director's role is to overlook almost every part of the filmmaking process. They are in charge of the film's creative vision and responsible for making all the major decisions involving the film.

Whilst you would normally have to organise and lead many different departments, explain

your vision and ensure the relevant
departments are taking the right steps to
achieve that vision - as you are essentially a
one person crew, this makes your job slightly
easier. You only have to explain your vision to
the actors, as almost all of the other work is
done solely by you, you just need to take the
necessary steps to ensure what you create is as
close as possible to what you originally
envisioned.

Assistant director

While it is the director's job to make all the
major decisions, the assistant director ('AD') is
responsible for the day to day running of the
shoot. They are in charge of the logistics, the
shooting schedule, they take care of the shot
list and liaise between the different
departments and the director. There can be
many different AD's, i.e. first AD, second AD,
third AD etc. depending on the scale of the
production.

On a limited-budget short film, you won't
have any departments, so this aspect of the
role is null and void. The one thing you will
have to do yourself is organise the running of

the shoot. This is made easier in pre production, if you create storyboards and a shot list. This will help you figure out timings and how long everything should take, from here you can deduce whether you are running on time or lagging behind.

Screenwriter

A screenwriter writes the initial draft of the script, and revises it based on suggestions from the director.

Please see the relevant screenplay chapter in this book, where this is discussed in more detail. However, if you choose to write your own script, you have full flexibility in revising it or deviating away from it when it comes to shooting.

Producer

It's quite difficult to narrow down a producer's role on a film set as it's incredibly broad. In fact, there are many different types of producers, such as executive producer, co-producer, associate producer, line producer etc. However, broadly speaking, a producer's

role is someone who helps to get the film
made. This can involve developing, planning,
co-ordinating the shooting process and
marketing the film. More specifically this can
include the following jobs, but bear in mind
that this isn't by any means an exhaustive list:

- Secure the rights to a project;
- Hire staff necessary to get the film
  made, including both cast and crew;
- Secure funds for the budget;
- Decide how the funds will be allocated;
- Overseeing the production schedule;
  and/or
- Marketing the film.

I would argue that a producer is a necessity on
a larger budget film, but a luxury on a short
low-budget film. Would it be easier to have a
producer who will take care of a lot of the film
making process? Absolutely. Is it necessary?
No.

As you are working on a much smaller scale,
you will most likely be using your own money
and therefore do not need to report to
investors or the such. This means you can set
your own production schedule and work to

your own timeline. It might take a bit more work, but you will also learn a lot more about the *business* of filmmaking, which requires a completely different skill set to the creative side of the business, yet can be just as important when it comes to becoming successful.

Location manager

A location manager helps scout possible locations which match the physical needs and feel of your film. They also ensure that these locations are safe for you and your staff to work in, as well as taking care of all the logistic requirements in relation to the site such as making sure there is adequate parking and electrical sockets. On top of this, they often are also involved in the pricing side and ensure that you get a good rate for the location.

While this is explained in further detail in other chapters in this book. For a short film, you should try and limit the number of locations your film is shot at to one or two. This will mean less work for you, as the more locations you are working at, the more work there will be initially (such as searching for locations) and the more things can will constantly require your attention and time.

The transportation department

This one is self-explanatory. Due to most films being set in multiple locations, most crews will have a transportation department whose sole purpose will be to transport the cast and crew from location A to location B.

As mentioned above, if you limit your short film to a single location, this will save on a number of costs, which includes the cost of transporting your cast and crew between locations. However, there are still ways around this. If you are shooting in different locations on different days, as long as the locations are not too far from each other and inconvenient to get to, there is nothing wrong with asking the cast and crew to meet you there. This is especially true if you are paying travel expenses.

Production manager

A production manager will make sure all the logistics of being on set are implemented in a timely and efficient fashion. They are responsible for creating a detailed schedule for the shoot and ensuring it is shot to budget. This is more of a business supervisor role, rather than a creative one.

On a short film, it is your responsibility to sit down and figure out what the production schedule should look like, how much time to allocate to each task and how you will pay for it. As most shoots will be a few days, at most, this shouldn't be a difficult or onerous task.

Cinematography department

Note that I am discussing the entire department in this section, rather than just the role of the main cinematographer, otherwise known as the Director of Photography.

Firstly, the role of the cinematographer is to capture the director's vision. They will use various cameras, lenses, lighting techniques, composition choices etc. in order to best tell the story and create a mood or feel for the story, which the director is trying to achieve. In order to achieve the look they require, they will rely on a number of different crew members, such as:

- Gaffers - responsible for the lighting on a film set;
- Grips - responsible for building and maintaining the equipment that supports the camera, such as a tripod, dolly, crane etc.
- Camera crew - responsible for operating the camera, swapping lenses, ensuring focus etc.

On a short film, you will most likely be operating the camera yourself. Most of the shots you will likely want to include in your film can probably be done using a fluid head tripod, a slider and a camera stabilizer of some sort, depending on your filmmaking style.

Lighting is a technical art that you will have to learn. As many online resources as there are, a lot of it comes down to trial and error, as well as using the available resources and space.

Better lighting can make more of a difference that an expensive camera.

Sound crew

Audio is half the movie going experience. It's what distinguishes amateurs from professionals.

During the shooting process, you will need to get clean audio of the dialogue, which can be done on a short film through using a shotgun microphone and/or using lavalier microphones. If you use a shotgun microphone attached to your camera or a boom pole and a lavalier microphone, you can record sound by yourself without a dedicated crew.

There will also be other sounds to consider depending on the nature of your short film, such as sound effects which can range from a dog barking on the street to an explosion. Luckily, a lot of sound effects are available to download free from various online resources, which keeps the budget down.

Script supervisor

A script supervisor's role is to oversee the
entire production, to ensure that there aren't
any continuity errors. This involves overseeing
the script, wardrobe, make up, set decoration
etc. They are there to prevent plot holes or
small errors which film geeks love to pick up
on. As films are often shot out of sequence,
with the director and cast often coming back
to do pick-up shots or scenes, after the initial
shoot, there can easily be confusion or errors
in the production. A script supervisor's role is
to prevent any of these errors from occurring.

What this translates to in your short film is
making sure you have an eye for detail. As
your shoot isn't as long, this should be slightly
easier. However, ensure that you create lists of
things that could potentially lead to errors so
you know what to look out for. Also, inspect
your footage closely during post production
and don't be afraid to reshoot scenes if the
error is very noticeable.

Digital intermediate technician

A Digital intermediate technician's ('DIT') role is to create backups of all the film recorded while on set. This is an underappreciated role which you should definitely not overlook.

I would recommend backing up your files at least twice per day. Once during the lunch break, to back up the morning's work and the second once every one has packed up to go home. There is nothing worse than losing footage and wasting all the time, money and energy it took in the first place. This is one of those lessons that isn't worth learning the hard way.

The Art Department

There are a number of roles which fall under this department, some of which I have listed below:

- Art director - The director oversees many of the roles listed below. They are responsible for making sure the characters, the props and fixtures and the environment and location helps

create the look and style the director
and cinematographer are trying to
achieve.

- Production/Set designer - The
  responsibility of a production/set
  designer is to ensure that the shooting
  location corroborates with the vision of
  the film. They will plan the design
  during the pre production phase and
  ensure it is executed as accurately as
  possible on the shooting days.

- Prop master - The property master will
  purchase or manufacture any props
  needed for production and then ensure
  the actors are informed on how to use
  them, and ensure their proper use and
  placement on set.

- Storyboard artist - The artist will
  visually create almost a comic like
  version of the script, in order to help
  break the director's vision of the script
  into pictures.

These are all roles which need consideration
when creating your short film. It is important,

for example, to consider how colours on your set align with your film's theme. Or whether placing a certain prop closer to character A than character B will influence the audience's perception of those characters. Be creative with your artistic choices, now is the time to experiment.

Hair, makeup and wardrobe

In order to keep the budget down, you can either learn these skills yourself and do the hair/makeup/wardrobe for your actors before you start shooting, or tell them to consider all of the above before they arrive.

The disadvantage to doing it yourself is that it is very time-consuming. Especially if you can only work with an actor for a set amount of hours, this will eat into your shooting hours, of which there are already never enough in a day.

Alternatively, asking the actors to consider the above before they arrive can be useful, as long as you are being reasonable. If the scene requires zombie makeup, this will cost the actor money to try and pull off accurately.

However, if it is just a guy dressed in a tracksuit, ask them if they have clothes they can use and bring along to the shoot. If your requirements are complex, you may need to consider either working with an up and coming makeup artist who wishes to gain experience on a film set or considering paying for a professional.

Of course there is the risk that if the actor's do the above by themselves that they will not follow your vision. The key here is *visual* communication. Send them pictures or videos of the looks you are going for as inspiration, rather than just trying to explain it. I've found that visual cues go much further in these areas.

Stunt coordinator

This may seem like a smaller role, which you may not have considered on a short film. I've mentioned the safety of your co-workers being the most important thing while you are shooting many times throughout this book. If you are planning to do any stunts, even if they do not appear to be dangerous, find someone who knows what they are doing. Do not play with people's safety. A stunt coordinator can ensure that the stunts are not only performed safely, but that they look the best that they can while you are filming.

Catering crew

Your cast and crew will expect to be fed. This is common in the industry, and you will be expected to feed them, especially if they are working for free or expenses only.

Catering can end up being surprisingly expensive. While big film sets can afford to hire dedicated chefs and mobile kitchens, this will not be an option for you. There are some cheaper options explained in the 'Production' chapter of this book.

Post production crew

Post-production is a huge part of the filmmaking process. Crew members involved in this department are responsible for colour grading, editing, sound mixing, creating the score etc.

There are free versions of post-production
colour grading, editing and sound mixing
software which can be found online. Some of
which are even competitive with paid
versions. There is a steep learning curve
involved and thus you have to dedicate some
time to learning how to properly apply these
skills and work around the software.
However, there are plenty of helpful sites and
tutorials online which make it a little easier.

CHAPTER 11: BE CREATIVE

Be creative

As a indie filmmaker, there are going to be many times where you are limited. The vast majority of these limitations will arise as a result of the low budget you are restricted to. However, there are ways to work around these restrictions by being creative and opting for D.I.Y. options. Whilst these may not be as high quality, they are a lot of fun, and part of the experience of being a filmmaker and director, is being able to solve problems with creative solutions. You are early on in your, hopefully, very long career - now is the time to have fun. Don't worry if you don't have the latest gadgets, it is your duty to be a filmmaker who can tell engaging stories and get astonishing shots, in spite of the low budget. Be creative, but most of all, have fun with it.

Equipment

If you are only just starting out, you may managed to get yourself a camera, or perhaps you are still using your smart phone. Either way, filmmaking is an expensive hobby/profession, and it takes time in building up a comprehensive set of filmmaking equipment. In the meantime, you may think that your short films will have to be limited as you don't have the latest tripod or gimbal to be able to get the same shots that your favourite Hollywood director is able to pull off. To a certain extent, this is true, there will be limitations. But like I said, don't be afraid to improvise.

Below are a list of replacements you could use until you find the funds to be able to purchase the equipment. Note that these are not exactly what we recommend you do, but are just alternatives we have used or seen used by other filmmakers, to inspire you that alternatives do exist.

- Tripods: There are two main types of
  tripods. A photography tripod which is
  stationary and can be used to lock
  down a certain frame and film either
  only what is in the shot, or zoom in or
  out with your camera to change the
  image. Alternatively, video tripods
  often have a fluid head meaning they
  can take 360 degree videos as the head
  of the tripod can be rotated. Fluid head
  video tripods are a little tricky to
  replicate, it can be done, but you need a
  certain level of DIY skills, however if
  you are happy to do so, there are plenty
  of tutorials online. In order to get the
  fixed tripod look, the easiest option is
  just to place your camera on an elevated
  surface and not move it during the
  entire shot. A camera will balance on its
  own, but if you are filmmaking with
  your phone, you can do something as
  simple as getting a used ice cream
  container (similar to Ben and Jerry's
  circular containers), cut some slits
  down the side to hold your camera, as
  well as one at the front so you can film.
  Then fill the container with some

weight, such as sand, so it doesn't topple and you're good to go.

- Slider: A slider is used to move the camera from one stationary point across smoothly to another. Again, there are plenty of tutorials online on creating really good DIY options, using cheaper materials. But if you're really just starting out, why not just place your camera on a towel, and slide it across a smooth surface like a kitchen top? Easy and free.

- Dolly: This is a piece of equipment which looks a bit like a little railway track, with a cart attached. The idea being that you can move your camera closer towards or away from the action. A simple DIY option for this is getting a friend or cast/crew member to push you on either a computer chair (with wheels) if you are shooting indoors or a shopping trolley if you are outdoors. The footage may be slightly shaky, but the more weight you add, the smoother the shot will be.

- Lights: Film lights can be pricey. And it's often justified too, as some of the new lights coming out can be adjusted for brightness through a smart phone, as well as adjusting the colour of the light which can help create a certain mood for your shot. While this is great for later in your career, while you are on a budget, the temptation is to use the lights in your house. The problem with this is that overhead lighting isn't very cinematic or flattering on your actors. Of course you can just use natural lighting and desk lamps, but what if you need something more powerful? Luckily, you can purchase really powerful LED garden lights at most DIY centres, which can replicate a professional LED film light.

- Light stand: Similar to a tripod, light stands can be replaced by just placing your light on every day elevated surfaces, like a chest of draws.

- Reflector: The problem with having such powerful lights is that you may get too bright an image. There are two ways around this, firstly you can buy a reflector to bounce the light off onto your actors, rather than shining it directly onto them. Or if you cannot afford this for the moment, get a large piece of cardboard and cover it with aluminium foil. You can use this is a makeshift reflector which does essentially the same thing.

- Soft light: Alternatively, if the light from your powerful LED lighting is too harsh, you would normally purchase a soft box, which as the name suggests will soften the light onto your subjects. The DIY alternative is to get a white bed cloth and draper it over your light. Make sure there is some space between the cloth and the light. Although LED lights are far less of a fire risk than traditional lights due to them advertised a being far less likely to overheat, it is best to be safe.

- Audio equipment: As mentioned in this book, audio equipment is super important when it comes to filmmaking. I would argue it is just as important as purchasing a camera. However, if you are literally just starting out and cannot afford to pay for any audio equipment, you can place a smart phone in your actor's pockets and use a voice recording app to record audio. Alternatively, purchase a lavalier microphone and plug this straight into a smart phone, this will not produce as good results as if you used a portable recorder device, however it is a good starting point.

Other hacks

Below are a list of easy tips and hacks which low budget filmmakers can use to improve the quality of their filming process. Not all of them will work for you, but try them out and see if you like any of them:

- To create a look of a fire flickering on your frame. Cut out both ends of a cylinder object, and use your phone to get a video of flickering and use this to aim towards your frame. Alternatively place a tablet (as it has a bigger screen), turned onto full screen brightness, into

a bucket to emulate a fire with the
flickering look. Your actors can then
throw paper into the bucket to make it
look as if they are burning it.

- If you are using cutlery in your scene,
  keep a jumper or something soft on the
  table which is just out of the frame, this
  will prevent your cutlery from making
  a clinking sound and interrupting your
  audio. This will save you time and cost
  in removing these sounds from post
  production.

- Label everything you have more than
  one of - lenses, spare batteries, cables
  etc. This will save you more time than
  you think, allowing you to work
  quicker.

- Second hand shops, charity shops and
  eBay should be your first port of call
  when it comes to purchasing props or
  clothes. Only buy new if you have to.

- If you are paying for a location, spend
  longer in rehearsal so you can cut down

the number of days you need to hire the
location for.

- Spend time finding the right actors. A
good actor will be able to give you a
good performance quicker, which can
not only save you money, but improve
the quality of your production
significantly.

- Always negotiate on every cost you are
expected to pay. It doesn't matter if this
is day rates, location rates, equipment
hire etc. Something is only worth what
you are willing to pay for it.

- Don't be afraid to borrow and ask for
favours. Built relationships by offering
to help others too and this will become
mutually beneficial, with more people
willing to help you in return.

- Put your own money up for your
projects. This way you will watch every
penny coming in and out and really
learn how to manage a budget and your
finances, which is a key skill in
filmmakers.

- Keep the film short. A 5 minute film will cost a lot less than making a 45 minute film. A longer film isn't necessarily a better one. It's how you use the time and structure the story that matters.

- When you are finished creating the final cut of your film, make sure you view it on several different devices such as a computer, laptop, tablet and phone - they will all look slightly different. Make sure you are happy with each.

- When you are sound mixing, check your audio levels with and without headphones. Make sure the audio is clear via both methods.

- Don't forget to make a poster for your film while you are on set! This can be a great marketing tool.

- Lastly, keep your expectations realistic. Your film isn't going to look like a Hollywood production. Indie filmmaking is an entirely different beast. At this stage of your career, treat your journey as a personal one. As long as you are improving from where you were in your last short film and still learning, you are on the right path.

CHAPTER 12: PRE-PRODUCTION

Pre production

Pre production is all the work that is necessary to ensure that you are ready and prepared for the actual shoot. It is easy to underestimate the amount of work that goes into pre production and leave yourself too little time to get everything done that you need to. Preparation is the key to a smooth shoot. Every problem that you solve in pre production is one less problem you will have to deal with when actually shooting the film. Your actual shoot will be time-pressured and there will inevitably be things that go wrong. As fun as shooting is, it can also be very stressful. By not preparing adequately, you are only making the actual shoot harder for yourself. So my advice would be to spend longer than you think you will need in pre production. You will thank yourself for it later down the line, believe me.

The first thing to do is take one final look at the script. Make sure it is finalised. This is the script which you will shoot. Ensure it is realistic within the shooting timeframe and with the limited resources you have available. Once your script is finalised, you are ready to begin pre production.

It is worth breaking down the script at this point, before you do anything else. This will help you figure out what resources you need. This way you know what resources you need to make sure your script can be brought to life. A good starting point is to make a list of the following:

- Props;
- Costumes;
- Locations;
- Crew;
- Actors;
- Extras;
- Makeup; and
- Filming/Audio equipment.

The script breakdown is a technical exercise. Do not worry about what you are experiencing in the story in terms of emotion etc. from a viewer's perspective. That should have all been finalised when you created the final working draft of your script.

Once you are happy with your scene breakdown, I would next go on to create a storyboard. A storyboard is a visual representation of your screenplay. Crudely put, it's how the scene would play it, if it was written up as a comic. It's incredibly useful to visualise how your scenes are going to play out, not just for yourself, but it is useful to share your vision with your cast and actors so they can gain a better understanding of the look you are trying to achieve. Do not worry if you're not great at drawing, a storyboard is functional, not an art piece. As long as you can get across key aspects of how you want your scene shot and framed, you can easily explain the other details to your cast and crew. If you are still unsure, have a look at storyboards online for films you have already watched.

If you are working with a cinematographer, you may also look into creating a mood board from similar movies to express the type of look you are going for, and the intended colour pallet of the movie. However, as you are unlikely to have a dedicated cinematographer at this stage of your career, I will leave out the detail from this.

Once you have a storyboard, depending on the complexity of your short film and how organised you tend to be as an individual, you may consider creating a shot list. A shot list is a summarised to do list for a day of shooting, which is often shared around with your crew to ensure nothing is forgotten. It is a reference point which you can use throughout your day to ensure you are staying on track. Things to include on a shot list are:

- Scene number;
- Location;
- Details of *how* you are planning to shoot the scenes (e.g. 2 medium shots from different angles, followed by a close up);
- Any character or camera movement involved;
- Action sequences;
- If dialogue is needed;
- Which actors are needed;
- Which props are needed;

- Which equipment is needed e.g. which lenses you will use; and
- Any special requirements of the scene.

Remember, that you do not have to include all of the above on a shot list. Just pick and choose the things most important to you. If you are unsure of what you will need, download a free shot list template from online for your first short film and adapt by it by adding things you would like to have remembered and taking away things which you don't feel you need, to tailor it to your needs.

A practical consideration you want to have whilst in pre production is how you are going to allocate the budget. The last thing you want to happen is to run out of money and not be able to pay the suppliers or staff you need. Create a budget at this stage and allocate all relevant costs to it. Keep it realistic, do not budget $10 for a location if you know they will not hire it out for less for $50 a day. If you have a producer, they would usually be in charge of the budget. But as you are unlikely to have one, the key things you may need to budget for are:

- Personnel - this includes actors, crew, writers, producers etc. Even if you aren't paying for their time, you should consider paying their expenses.

- Production costs - these include props, technical equipment (e.g. camera, audio etc.), locations, permits, electricity, insurance etc.

- Post-production costs - This is usually labour, subscriptions (e.g. to video editing software), facilities etc.

- Marketing - this is only applicable if you are planning to advertise your short film and will include advertising costs, legal costs and festival fees.

It is always worth keeping a small surplus of cash, say an extra 10% of the movie's budget, in case you have a light bulb moment and want to add in an extra prop or do something which costs slightly more but will make all the difference to your film. Or in case any of your props are damaged and need replacing or a location is cancelled last minute.

I cannot recommend double checking your budget at least three or four times over to make sure it is realistic and that there are no arithmetic errors. You do not want to be caught short.

The next thing to do is to gather all your resources. This includes picking out your locations and blocking out a date, getting all the wardrobe and props ready, hiring your actors and crew, getting all the equipment ready etc. It is imperative at this stage that everyone knows what their role is, there should not be any confusion as to who is expected to do what. Communication is key. Everyone should be told about their individual role, what it expected of them, and how this fits into the larger aspect of the film. Setting clear expectations of yourself and your peers at this stage will prevent confusion at later stages, which can easily build into frustration and resentment, especially if the shoot is stressful anyway.

Create a schedule of what needs to be done and when it needs to be done by. Plan out each and every stage, almost on a day by day

basis. This way you will know whether you
are on target to complete a film by a certain
date. I've seen far too many filmmakers do all
the really interesting work of planning and
shooting a film, and then dragging their heels
for months, and sometimes even years, when
it comes to doing the post production aspect.
Set yourself targets or it's easy to let things
slip.

Scheduling also helps to work around other
people's lives. For example, if you have set a 5
day period for your main shoot, one of your
actors may only be available for the first 3
days. While this may initially seem like a deal
breaker, as long as you are aware of this in
advance, you can schedule all their scenes
earlier in the shoot. This can save time as you
won't need to recast someone else for the role.

One of the main things that filmmakers skip
over when making a short film is rehearsals. I
cannot stress enough how valuable these are.
It is easy to dismiss rehearsing when the script
is perhaps only 5 pages long, as it is easy to
rationalise that you can just do a quick
rehearsal on the day, before you begin
shooting. And while this is true, you will not

have the added benefit of being able to take away the footage and spend a few days thinking about what could be improved. It is also a great opportunity to get to know the actors, their style and working out how you can work in a more collaborative and constructive way with them, in order to get the most out of their performances. Moreover, if the actors have met you and each other beforehand, they are more likely to be comfortable and therefore give more open performances. An actor can only give their best performance when they are comfortable knowing that they have a safe space to be vulnerable. Rehearsals are the ideal time to build this rapport.

Of course you are trying to create this short film on a budget, so I would not recommend hiring a separate rehearsal space. Rehearsals are meant to be informal so a dedicated space isn't really necessary. Most actors will be happy to rehearse in either your apartment or theirs. If you are only working with a single actor, do it virtually if you really don't want to spend money reimbursing them, however I would not recommend this for shoots with more than a single actor.

CHAPTER 13:
PRODUCTION

Production

By the time you get to the production stage, where you are ready to shoot your film, you should have already forked up almost all of the costs necessary to do the shooting, at the pre production stage. For example, if you require your actors to shoot at a set location or to have a set wardrobe, you will already have paid for this during pre production. All you need to do during shoot days is to turn up with the equipment, props, wardrobe etc. right?

Contingency cash

Well, almost. I would recommend still leaving a small amount in your budget for things you may need to "top up" at this stage. I call this having 'contingency cash'. There are two main times you may need to inject some extra cash into your film at the production stage.

Firstly, things will get lost or damaged. This is just a fact. Whether this is through the continuous use of props, or one of your actors accidently spills some bolognaise sauce on his tailored outfit during one of the lunch breaks. These things just happen, and there is no way to plan for accidents. If you have a small amount of contingency cash available during such events, it just takes the stress off. You don't have to halt production, considering where you can source a replacement for free, you just fork out slightly and continue shooting as normal.

The other instance where having contingency cash is an advantage is if you decide to deviate from the script, and need an extra prop. As an example, if you are working on a short film within the comedy genre, one of your actors may decide to improvise the scene and actually come up with a line which is much funnier than what you had originally written in the script. But to make the joke work, he or she may need a cheap prop. If it is really going to improve the scene, you do not want to be in a position where you can't spare any money towards it. In this instance, it is worth dipping your hand into the contingency cash fund.

Expenses

It is not very often that in a book about how to do something for as cheap as possible, you are advised on how you should spend money. I know the below list will seem like unnecessary expenses, however it is worth considering paying out for them. Technically you can make your short film without them, so consider the below as recommended, yet optional, extra costs.

First of all, consider whether you should pay expenses for your actors and crew. From a purely commercial point of view, this will benefit your production as you will get a wider range of applicants. If people know that there travel expenses are covered, they are more likely to apply, thus meaning that you have more choice when deciding which actor(s) should play the role(s) in your film. The more choice, the higher the chance of finding a better fit for the role, which in turn could elevate your short film from an amateur

wannabe student film to an engaging film
which audiences cannot take their eyes off.

Moreover, there is argument for paying
expenses to ensure that your cast and crew are
not out of pocket. They are helping to bring
your vision to life, it could be argued that it is
your responsibility to cover the cost for this.
Furthermore, offer new actors the chance to
use the footage as part of their show reel.
Creating a good experience for actors which is
mutually beneficial will give you a good
reputation in the industry, you will be more
likely to work with the same actors again, as
well as be recommended to their fellow
colleagues.

Catering

Another cost which you may consider
unnecessary is catering costs. It is true that in
almost every other profession and industry on
the planet, staff are expected to bring their
own food in for lunch, this is not provided by
their employer. However, the industry
expectation for the film industry is that lunch
is provided, and/or dinner if you are working
later in the evening or doing a night shoot.

There are many different ways you can source your meals, the options (running from cheapest to most expensive) are:

- Homemade food - don't be afraid to get cooking. This will be the cheapest method. Bulk buy a cheap staple like pasta, and make your own bolognaise or tomato sauce to go with it. Most actors will be appreciate of homemade food, if it is done right. This is also the method used by many director's when they were still making independent productions. Famously, Quentin Tarantino's cast and crew used to love coming to set on My Best Friend's Birthday as his mum used to home cook delicious food for them all.

- Buying food from supermarkets - pick up a 'meal deal' or a group of pre-made sandwiches for the cast and crew. Whilst not the most exciting option, this is probably the best blend of convenience and price.

- Getting takeaways - this isn't the healthiest option, nor the cheapest. However, if your set is not close to your home or a supermarket, this can be an easy and convenient way to get in a hot meal.

- Going to restaurants - This is definitely one of the most expensive options and is not sustainable financially in the long term. However, if you are doing a one day shoot, this could be a nice way to treat your cast and crew for doing a great job.

- Using a dedicated catering company - This is one of the most expensive long-term options, as you usually pay a premium for pre-made meals which are delivered to you. However, it takes all the thinking out of it. If you want a hassle free option, this is it.

Regardless of which option you choose, keep it efficient. Do not order more food than you need, in case anyone has a huge appetite. Assume a standard portion for everyone, and don't anticipate leftovers, unless you can take them home for your dinner or people are happy to tuck into them the following day.

Don't forget to ask around for allergy information if you are providing food. This is not a preference, treat allergies very seriously and ensure there is no cross-contamination.

Don't forget to also offer drinks throughout the day. Your team will not perform well if they are not well looked after. This can either just be water, or also extended to hot drinks, such as tea and coffee. Don't forget to include sugar, sweeteners, dairy and non dairy milk etc.

Whether you choose to offer snacks is up to you. Some directors don't offer sugary snacks, due to the high and come down's associated with it and needing to keep a certain level of energy on set.

Insurance

I have mentioned this continuously throughout this book, but I can't stress it enough, get some sort of insurance to cover yourself and your team in case something goes south. No one thinks it is going to happen to them, until it does. Don't ruin your reputation so early in your career as being the director that compromised his/her team's safety to save a few dollars. It simply isn't worth it.

CHAPTER 14: THE SCORE

Score

Music is an extremely effective tool when it comes to shaping the audience's experience. Often, as filmmakers, our role is to influence the audience's emotions within a particular scene in order to make them feel or react in a particular way, for example it is the director's role to terrify the audience during a scene involving a jump scare within a horror film. Music is a fantastic way to evoke a certain emotion within the audience.

Furthermore, music can help link certain parts of a story together and make it easier to piece together for the audience. For example, if your story involves certain cyclical elements, then using the same melodies every time these events occur can help remind the audience of the pattern they should be observing.

Therefore, music can also help the story flow more coherently for the audience.

Another great use of music is being able to create a specific atmosphere for the audience in relation to a specific time period. For example, if you are making a movie about Sweden in the 1970's, using music from the pop group ABBA could help transport the audiences mind frame to that particular period. Similarly, using music from a different time period can help take the audience out of the illusion. As an example, many people criticized the use of Jay Z's music in Baz Luhrmann's The Great Gatsby as the movie is set during the 1920's, they argued that hearing such contemporary music in a classical tale took them out of the experience. Although, it depends on how the music is incorporated into the movie. For instance, Quentin Tarantino's use of a Rick Ross song in Django Unchained was praised by some, despite the movie being set in the 1600's as it added to the feeling of the scene. It is down to your creative input as to whether adding time relevant music is best for your movie.

Although this chapter regarding music is placed towards the end of the book, this does not necessarily mean that you should start considering music towards the end of your filmmaking process. There is no right or wrong way to approach this, it is down to the personal preference of the director. Some directors like to think about music very early on in the process, take Quentin Tarantino for example, who likes to write his scenes to music. This can help to figure out the rhythm and feel of the scene and you are able to structure the dialogue and actions in the best way around the music which can lead to incredibly memorable scenes, which are associated with a piece of music. One of Quentin Tarantino's most iconic scenes is in fact one he had written to with a piece of music in mind, which is the famous scene in Reservoir Dogs which is written to Stuck In The Middle With You by Stealers Wheel. Alternatively, there are other famous directors, such as Sidney Lumet, who added music only after the editing of their final version of the film was complete. They considered adding music as enhancing what they had already achieved. The main benefit of this approach is that the music will not influence the actual story, but rather enhance it, leaving the actual story to be more powerful in its own right.

If you are licensing music which someone else has created, you will need to pay royalties over to whoever owns the rights to the music. This can be incredibly costly, especially if it's a well known piece. Following on from the example above, Quentin Tarantino has talked about how he used the entire $13,000 music budget for Reservoir Dogs on Stuck In The Middle With You. He was forced to pay this amount as he had written the scene to that piece of music. The lesson to learn from here is to not write scenes in your short film to well known, popular music.

Well, what's a workaround for this? One option is to create your own music. This is ideal for those who already own a musical instrument and have a musical background. It is the perfect way to tailor your music to your scenes and evoke the specific emotion intended from your audiences. Although, most of you will run into limitations with this method as you may want more than one musical instrument throughout your short.

However, this doesn't mean you cannot compose at least part of the score yourself.

For those of you who would love to create an original soundtrack, but do not have the ability to play a musical instrument, there are many music production packages online. These enable you to create a multi instrument track from your PC, which you can download and add to your short film. Of course you will need to have a musical ear, but if you are so inclined, this is a great way to create an original soundtrack for free.

If you are not musically inclined, there are also many websites which provide royalty free music, which you can then add to your short film. If you are potentially looking to monetise on your film, it is important to make sure that the music you are licensing has a clause which allows commercial use. Also, make sure that you always link back and give some sort of credit to the website and artist(s) who created the music in the first place.

Alternatively, work with an up and coming music composer who is trying to break into the film industry. The advantage of going for this option is that they are likely to be just as passionate about the creative side of the process as you are, and therefore you can explain how to shape the original score based on the themes of the short film and the emotions the scene is supposed to evoke. You also have the option of revising the score continuously, within reason, until it fits the beat of your film. Amateur film composers can be found online, or at film schools. If you end up having a great experience with the composer, this will also make it easier to build an original score for your future films, as long as you are both happy to continue working together.

Lastly, if you are after songs with vocals added by a singer(s), then your best choice may be to look for local singers or bands in your area. This can involve friends or family. Alternatively, if you do not know anyone, reach out to a local band or artist who creates original music and ask if you can use their music, perhaps in exchange for a credit in your short film.

CHAPTER 15: EDITING

Editing

*Editing is where movies are made or broken. Many
a film has been saved and many a film has been
ruined in the editing room.*
- Joe Dante

Films are made three times. Once as a
literature piece in the form of a script,
secondly when they are being shot and being
bought to life on camera and finally a film is
remade in the editing room. Whilst the initial
two forms inform the third, the third is
arguably the most important as it is the only
draft that the audience gets to see. It is a well
known anecdote in the film community that
Star Wars: A New Hope was saved in the
editing room by Paul Hirsch. This is not a
knock on the rest of the cast or crew, but
signifies the importance of a good editor.
Whilst George Lucas provided Paul with

fantastic footage, Paul's decision to delete certain scenes, restructure the story in an engaging way and dictating the pace and rhythm of the movie is what turned it into the classic it is known as today.

Software

Before I begin on the post production editing process, most of you will probably be thinking that whilst post production is important and necessary, it can also be hugely expensive. And you're right, it can be. However, for the purpose of your short film, as long as you are willing to take the time to learn, you can also do it yourself for free. Of course you are unlikely to reach the same standard as those who edit professionally for a living, there is a reason why their day rates are so expensive, it is incredibly skilled work. However, you can still edit well enough for the purposes of creating a short film. You may not be able to use advanced VFX, but you can cut different footage together, colour grade and sound mix to tell an engaging narrative story.

There are plenty of free post production editing software online. Some of which is the

basic version of more advanced software
which you have to pay for, and other options
are open-source free software which is
constantly updated and free to all. Play
around with a few different options and use
what is best for you. You will spend a lot of
time editing, so choose an option you are
happy with. I would recommend choosing
software which gives you the option to cut
and merge footage, colour grade and mix
audio and sound all in one package rather
than downloading different software packages
for each task. I find it easier to do all my
editing in one package rather than trying to
cut back and forth between different types of
software, but again, do what works for you.

As a disclaimer, video editing software tends
to be very intensive on your computer's CPU
and requires a strong graphics card. If you are
working off a lower end laptop, you either
may need to upgrade or you will be limited in
your choice of which software to use.
However, in the age where you are able to edit
even through your smart phone, there are no
excuses.

There are many post production processes involving sound, most of which was discussed in the dedicated sound chapter of this book. Therefore they are discussed only briefly below, for more detail, please refer to the relevant chapter:

- ADR: This stands for Automatic Dialog Replacement and refers to actors re-recording their dialogue for a scene in post production, with the intention that it is synchronised with the footage and replaced with the original sound. This is usually done as the original sound recorded was of too low a quality to be used in the film.

- Foley: Foley is the recording of everyday sounds in post production which add a more realistic feel to the film. These can include recording original sound in post production for a more clear sound, such as footsteps. Or recreating sounds for actions where getting original sound is not an option,

such as breaking celery to replicate the
sounds of broken bones.

- Sound effects: These are usually larger
  than life noises, such as explosions,
  which are usually taken from pre-
  recorded online databases.

The other aspect of sound production is sound
mixing. The first step is to synchronise the
sound you have recorded to the footage. This
is especially important if you were recording
sound using a dual recording system, such as
a lavalier microphone recording the actual
sound and an external shotgun microphone
recording the reference sound. You should be
easily able to replace the reference sound with
the clean sound by looking for the point where
you used the clapper, which will give you a
spike in the audio waveform which you can
use as a reference point for the replacement.

With sound mixing, you also need to make
sure that the volume is mixed well between all
the different sources of sound. As an example,
Christopher Nolan is constantly criticized for
the music being too loud in his films, to the
point where you struggle to hear the dialogue.

Nolan has come out and said that this is an intentional artistic choice for him. However, you have to consider what the right balance is between the volume of your dialogue, soundtrack and sound effects.

It is also tempting as a new filmmaker to overdo it with foley and sound effects, and add these to literally every part of the film. This is not only time consuming but can be detrimental to the film. This is because it can take away from how "real" the scenario feels. It can make the audience aware that they are watching a film, rather than being immersed in the experience. Again, experiment with the amount of additional sound effects you add in post production, until you get the right effect that you are looking for.

Footage

You will have recorded a lot more footage than you actually need to include the final cut of the short film. This is because you will have recorded the scenes from many different angles, such as a master shot, a medium shot and a close up of your actors. On top of this, you should have plenty of footage of what is essentially B-roll, being supplemental footage, perhaps close up shots of props or footage of the location etc. which you can intersperse into your main footage to help give the audience context, focus the audience's attention on something or to add a certain feel to the film.

Unsurprisingly, the first thing you will need to do is to watch all of the footage. This can be a long and tedious task, but it is absolutely necessary to do so. This is a great way to remind yourself of what you have shot, and see it properly for the first time since you have shot the footage. Just by going through the footage, you should be able to eliminate some of the footage, purely on technical grounds as you will undoubtedly have footage which may be out of focus or too shaky to even fix in post production. This will limit the amount of footage you can choose from. Some of the technically poor footage may be some of your favourite shots, this happens to everyone. You can either rerecord it or move on, do not use poor footage in your final cut, it looks unprofessional.

You will probably spend a significant amount of time in deciding what footage you will actually like to keep for your final cut. Plan in this time if you have got a specific deadline for your short film, such as a film festival. This process always takes longer than anticipated. When deciding which footage to use, there are a few things to consider:

- The narrative: Let's start with an example of the opening shot of the film. If your film is set in a single location, being an abandoned warehouse, your film may start with a wide shot of the warehouse exterior, so your audience knows where the film is set. It may then move into a wide shot of the characters within the warehouse disposal area, before moving into a medium shot of the two lead characters, who are dressed in waste disposal uniform, engaging in dialogue. By framing the story this way, we know where the story is set (a warehouse), which part of the warehouse the leads work in (waste disposal), before moving into the actual dialogue. Through three simple shots, the audience can gauge the context of the story. The narrative should inform which shots you use and what information you want revealed to the audience in which order.

- The theme: The theme will have influenced how you shot the film, and these type of decisions should continue into the editing room. If you are making a short film with the main theme being that of loneliness, you may decide to use more wide shots in the final cut of the film, to show the emptiness around the main character.

- Angles: You may have shot the same footage from a number of different angles and focal lengths. Sometimes it is just a case of picking whatever looks more aesthetically pleasing, or works best with the other footage that you have available.

- B-roll: the B-roll you use will depend on which shots are corrupted and therefore need replacing with secondary footage, or whether you want to draw your audience's attention to something in particular.

Consider which order you wish to place your footage in. It is tempting to always tell your story in a linear, chronological fashion. However, sometimes by throwing the footage out of order, you can actually tell the story in a more engaging way and keep the audience guessing and engaged, especially if you are working in a crime or thriller genre. Certain directors, like Christopher Nolan, have built their careers and reputations on being able to narrate a story in a non-linear fashion. For example, if you watch a film like Dunkirk which jumps back and forth between the stories of the different characters and the different time periods, and try and rearrange it to a more linear fashion, it just isn't able to achieve the same intense effect that it does being told in a non-linear order. Don't feel afraid to cut back and forth between two separate storylines, between intertwining them together, revealing bits of information at a time. Finding the voice of the story can take time and may even be a trial and error process, where you make two separate edits of the film, one in chronological order and a separate version which is more experimental in its story telling style.

The editing room is also where you are able to dictate the pace of your film. By cutting back and forth between short clips, you can create a more fast paced film which keeps the audience's eyes constantly moving across the screen, trying to figure out what is going on. Alternatively, by using incredibly long shots which carry on for minutes at a time, you can create a more slow or claustrophobic atmosphere where the audience is unable to escape. The pace of the film should be dictated by the theme and genre of the film.

Remember that not only the length of the shots, but also the editing techniques will affect the pace and feel of the film. For example, the way the film fades in or the choice of transitions between shots will inform how it is viewed.

This will also inform choices, which may at first appear to be technical decisions, but an element of creativity should also be used. For example, an important part of the editing process is colour grading. Most filmmakers will choose to shoot in a "dull" setting on their camera, where all the colours are slightly faded. This is because it is then easier to colour grade in post production, it gives a wider range of choice and allows for a better finish on the final cut. Whilst colour grading does involve making the footage look more cinematic and aesthetically pleasing (I mean who doesn't love a beautiful shot?), it should also compliment the theme of the film. As a simplified example, if the character is in a situation where they are feeling warmth towards another character, you may choose to colour grade towards more of an orange colour, rather than blue and cold. Audiences associate certain colours towards certain emotions, and this is just another tool to use as a filmmaker which can help manipulate the audience and the way you want them to feel.

Another artistic choice, which has been discussed before, so I will only speak on briefly is the soundtrack. The choice of music and the way in which you insert music and for how long will influence audience emotion and should be used with thought.

Rinse and repeat

After completing the final cut of your film, you should always watch it back, kick your feet up and pat yourself on the back. Congratulations, you are done.

...Well, not quite.

It is easy to get lost in the footage and not be able to look at it objectively when you have been editing the same footage for weeks or months on end. This will create blind spots, where you cannot tell where you should be adding in certain footage or taking certain footage away, changing the pace of the footage, changing your transitions etc.

The best way to get around this, I have found, is to watch the final cut with a small audience. For some reason, this gets you to view the film as an audience member, rather than an editor. This fresh perspective will allow you to make some minor adjustments to your film, which will make it more audience friendly. You can also get feedback from your target audience and take their suggestions on board. Though remember, there is a fine line between

accepting another person's suggestions and
compromising on your own vision.

Rinse and repeat this process until you are
happy with your film. Only then are you done.

CHAPTER 16:
MARKETING AND DISTRIBUTION

Marketing and Distribution

While there are countless advantages to creating short films, two of the main ones I listed during the introduction to this book were the learning process and the marketing aspect. The majority of this book has been focused on teaching the process of creating a short film and what can be learnt when developing one's style. The other main advantage is the opportunity short films give to help build an audience or following, and create a name for yourself as a filmmaker. This can help bring you on the radar of casual or potential diehard fans, helping build relationships with colleagues within the filmmaking community or even amongst those in the corporate filmmaking community who may help you in the future to build a career.

There are plenty of real life examples of filmmakers who have come up making amateur short films, and sometimes even amateur feature films, and later gone on to have an incredibly successful career in the global film market, with their amateur productions helping them and provide them with the platform they needed to get noticed. In order to prove that making short films can lead to a successful career, below are a number of brief case studies of a few incredibly successful director's getting their start through short films:

<u>Steven Spielberg</u>

When you think about amateur filmmakers who are filming low budget short films, you don't think about someone as iconic as Steven Spielberg, arguably one of the greatest directors of all time, being in the same position you are in now. After dropping out of California State University, Spielberg made a silent short film called Amblin. It was based on the quality of this short film that it caught the attention of Sid Sheinberg, the vice

president of production for Universal
Television, who offered Spielberg a seven year
contract to the studio, thus launching his
professional career. And the rest was history.

<u>George Lucas</u>

I know what you're thinking. The guy who
made Star Wars got his start making short
films? It is absolutely true, even the most
commercially successful director of all time
started out as an amateur short film director.
Having been a film student at multiple
universities, Lucas started out making a
number of short films, which include Freiheit,
Look at Life and Herbie. However, it wasn't
until he made a short film called Electronic
Labyrinth: THX 1138 4EB that he gained
recognition by winning first prize at the
1967/68 National Student Film Festival. The
concept for this short film would then go on to
serve as the premise of his first feature film,
titled THX 1138. A great lesson from Lucas'
story is that you may have to continue making
a number of short films before you are
recognised, do not expect overnight success,
but continue to create and eventually you will
break through.

Tim Burton

Tim Burton has one of the most unique styles of film in Hollywood. He first explored his unique storytelling and content through his short film Stalk of the Celery Monster, while he was a student at The California Institute of Arts. He then went on to make many other short films, which proved out to be so successful that they created a buzz around him, until he was eventually on the radar of Disney Animation Studios, who approached him for an apprenticeship.

Paul Thomas Anderson

Paul Thomas Anderson is widely regarded as one of Hollywood's most signature auteur filmmakers, who writes and directs films in his own unique way. Anderson started out creating a short film when he was 17 years old called The Dirk Diggler Story. If the name sounds familiar, it's because it helped form the basis of his infamous second feature film, Boogie Nights. Anderson eventually dropped out of film school and took all the money he had (as well as borrowing money from others) to make a short film called Cigarettes and

Coffee, which served as his own personal film school, which helped get him recognition as he earned a place at the Sundance's Directors Lab at the infamous Sundance Film Festival. This would not have been possible if he didn't possess the passion and resourcefulness to put himself out there and use what resources he had to make a short film. Anderson decided that being a content creator was more useful to helping him become a filmmaker, than the traditional formal learning path of film school. This is not to say that you shouldn't attend film school if you are considering this as an option, but just highlighting the value of putting yourself out there and the amount you can learn through just creating original content.

Christopher Nolan

Nolan has famously made a number of short films including Larceny, Tarantella and Doodlebug. The latter which explores themes such as time and reality manipulation, which he explores continually throughout his career. However, it wasn't until Nolan funded his first feature film 'Following', where he started to get international recognition. This would go on to launch his career. The inspiring thing about Nolan's first feature is that it was entirely self funded, at an estimated amount of only $6,000. Proving to everyone that it is possible to launch your own career, with the right passion and resourcefulness.

Release

Short films do not really have an income generating market. Theatres will not show short films, and unless you are already an incredibly successful director, it is unlikely that streaming services will want to pay for your short film. Almost all short films are released on video platforms for free, with the aim of building an audience and fan base. Your aim with the release of the short film should be to get as many people to see it as possible. Hopefully it will gain enough traction to be noticed by someone in the corporate filmmaking industry, but even if it is not, you can still begin to create an audience for yourself. I would recommend trying to upload the short film to as many video hosting platforms as possible. This gives you the chance to reach as wide an audience as possible.

There are many ways in which you can market and promote your short film, which are discussed below. However, there are also a few things you can do on the video hosting platform to help attract viewers to your short film.

Firstly, you can release a teaser or a trailer for your film. Personally, I am not a fan of releasing teasers for short films as this seems like overkill. Your trailer should less than a minute long, ideally even half this time, due to how short your film is going to be. Remember that a trailer should not reveal the entire plot of the film, but just give your audience enough of a taste that they should long for more.

The other type of video you can release as promotional material is behind the scenes footage. Not only is this a great way to attract fellow filmmakers to your short film, but it is invaluable to the film community. Fellow filmmakers will be extremely keen to learn from your short film, in regards to both what went well and what you felt like you could improve on if you were to repeat the process. They may even reach out to you for help and advice, thus helping you form invaluable relationships within the amateur filmmaking community.

Marketing

A few decades ago, it was a lot more difficult to market a short film, especially if you were working with practically next to no budget. You would have to hire out a billboard, make flyers or advertise on the TV or radio. Nowadays, thanks to the rise of social media, you can reach a huge audience through the comfort of your home, without spending a single penny. Granted that it is difficult to build a following, though there are short cuts through paid advertisements, if you do not have the timeline or patience to build an organic audience. You should share details of your short film through not only your own social media, on as many platforms as you can, but also request that your friends, family, cast and crew members also share your posts. This is an easy way of leveraging your relationships in order to reach as many people as possible.

If you are not social media savvy, a great way
to reach an audience through social media is to
partner up with influencers. These are
individuals, for our purposes ideally within
the filmmaking community, who already have
a strong social media presence, with a loyal
fan base, to which you can pitch your short
film. Most influencers will ask for some sort of
monetary payment to promote your short film.
If you are not willing or able to pay, there are
still a few alternatives. One option is to barter
with the influencer, while you cannot make a
payment, you can offer your video editing (or
other similar) services for their next 5 videos
or so, for free, in exchange for a single post on
one of their social media platforms. An
alternative way of getting influencers on board
is to cast them in your film. This way they will
more than willing to share the short film on
their platform, as it's also great promotion for
them personally.

Another way to market your films through the
comfort of your own home is to start a blog.
Only do this if you are going to be consistent
with it and will actually enjoy the process.
Creating a successful blog is not just a case of
creating a few articles and waiting for an

audience to reach you. The competition in this space is fierce. You will most likely be writing multiple articles a week for months or even years before you begin to gain some traction. This is definitely a long term strategy.

However, if this is the route you choose to go down, then this allows the opportunity to create a marketing list (make sure you read up on GDPR guidance if you choose to go down this route). Having a list of potential viewers is a fantastic way to ensure your short films will always have a solid foundational audience when you initially roll them out.

The alternative to social media is using more traditional media outlets as a source of marketing. The main advantage to this is that you may be able to reach a certain demographic which social media does not cover, for example many of the older generation never got bitten by the social media bug however they still use traditional media outlets. While you cannot afford to place advertisements on national media platforms, many small, local radio stations and newspapers or magazines will be happy to speak to a local filmmaker, if you reach out.

It's always worth asking, the worse they can say is no, in which case you have not lost anything.

The last form of marketing is perhaps the oldest form and many would argue, the most effective. A lot of films gain traction based on word of mouth marketing, which is just people talking about it. You can start this off by talking to your friends and family and hopefully they will do the same with their network. If your film is any good, this can snowball in a massive way.

Film festivals

During the case studies section of this chapter, a few of the directors mentioned had started out making a short film and only getting noticed once their film had been played at a film festival.

Film festivals can be expensive, especially well known top-tier festivals, which can cost hundreds of dollars to enter, with no guarantee that your film will ever be shown.

So the age old question is - are film festivals worth applying to for short films? Well, it depends. The first thing to note is that not all film festivals are created equal. There are tonnes of small, local film festivals which only receive a handful of entrants, which virtually no one pays attention to. In this case, there is not much advantage to entering. For the price of your entrance fee, you are better off putting this money into your next project. On the other extreme end of the scale, the competition for the largest film festivals is so intense that the chance of winning, especially when competing with small films which have budgets of millions of dollars, is miniscule. You need to find a balance.

My advice would be to enter a film festival only if you think your short film is of good enough quality to potentially win. If not, save your money and create another short film, and another, and another etc. until you create one which you feel is good enough to win. Only enter film festivals where you know there will be a network of other filmmakers, agents, distributors etc. that you want to network with. As there is no guarantee of winning, the least you want to do is attend the festival and use it as a networking opportunity to help create relationships that you can leverage in the future.

Research. Research. Research. Only enter film festivals which suit your style and genre of filmmaking, and are legitimate competitions which can help launch your career. Getting noticed by distributors and agents at a festival can help launch your professional career, but only if your film is good enough.

CHAPTER 17: FINAL THOUGHTS

Final Thoughts

Finally, we would like to thank each and every one of you who has made it this far into the book. We hope that you have found that book both informative and entertaining to read. Use the tips in this book as a guide, rather than advice that *must* be followed. Use what you want to inform your own unique style and voice as a filmmaker, and feel free to disregard or change some the advice to better suit your own needs. It is worth noting that the teachings of this book are not just meant to be read, but applied. So go out there and make your dream into a reality. Don't be scared to learn, and most importantly, don't be afraid to fail time and time again. It doesn't matter if your first few short films suck, chances are that they probably will. Enjoy the process. Filmmaking is the most fun craft in the entire world. And remember, making a film on a

budget is not an excuse for poor behaviour
when negotiating or an excuse to treat staff
poorly. As a director, it is your responsibility
to ensure everyone involved in the filmmaking
process leaves having had a positive
experience.

Once again, thank you for your support in
purchasing this book. As a small business,
each and every sale is appreciated.

If you have any questions on anything
mentioned in this book or related to
filmmaking, or alternatively if you wish to
share your journey with us or simply wish to
follow our journey, we would love to hear
from you at:

www.rizanproductionhouse.com

And lastly, please, please, please leave us a
review on **Amazon**, as it helps us to grow.